Abraham Lincoln

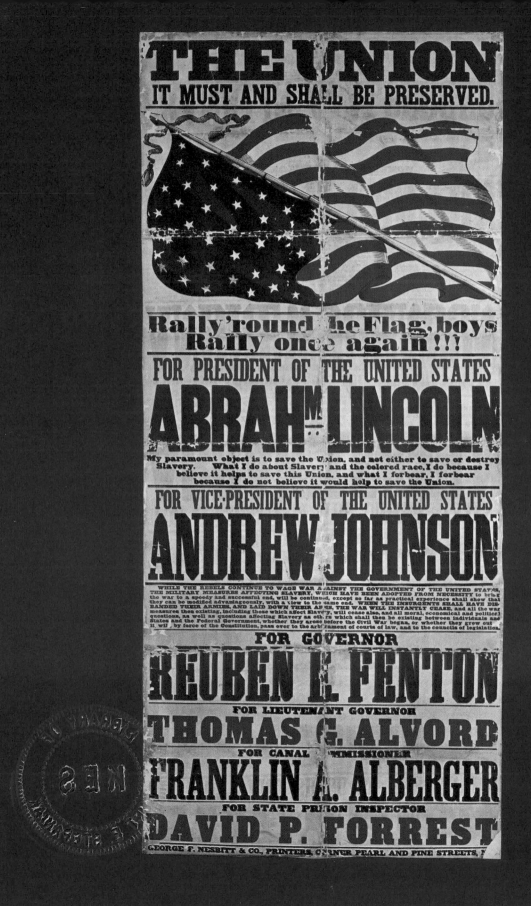

THE UNION
IT MUST AND SHALL BE PRESERVED.

Rally 'round the Flag, boys
Rally once again!!!

FOR PRESIDENT OF THE UNITED STATES
ABRAH^M LINCOLN

My paramount object is to save the Union, and not either to save or destroy Slavery. What I do about Slavery and the colored race, I do because I believe it helps to save this Union, and what I forbear, I forbear because I do not believe it would help to save the Union.

FOR VICE-PRESIDENT OF THE UNITED STATES
ANDREW JOHNSON

WHILE THE REBELS CONTINUE TO WAGE WAR AGAINST THE GOVERNMENT OF THE UNITED STATES, THE MILITARY MEASURES AFFECTING SLAVERY, WHICH HAVE BEEN ADOPTED FROM NECESSITY to bring the war to a speedy and successful end, will be continued, except so far as practical experience shall show that they can be modified advantageously, with a view to the same end. WHEN THE INSURGENTS SHALL HAVE DISBANDED THEIR ARMIES, AND LAID DOWN THEIR ARMS, THE WAR WILL INSTANTLY CEASE, and all the war measures then existing, including those which affect Slavery, will cease also, and all moral, economical and political questions, as well as questions affecting Slavery as others which shall then be existing between individuals and States and the Federal Government, whether they arose before the Civil War began, or whether they grew out it will, by force of the Constitution, pass over to the arbitrament of courts of law, and to the councils of legislation.

FOR GOVERNOR
REUBEN E. FENTON
FOR LIEUTENANT GOVERNOR
THOMAS G. ALVORD
FOR CANAL COMMISSIONER
FRANKLIN A. ALBERGER
FOR STATE PRISON INSPECTOR
DAVID P. FORREST

GEORGE F. NESBITT & CO., PRINTERS, CORNER PEARL AND PINE STREETS,

Abraham Lincoln

Lord Longford

Introduction by Elizabeth Longford

G.P. Putnam's Sons. New York

To Elizabeth

First American Edition 1975

© George Weidenfeld and Nicolson Limited
and Book Club Associates 1974

Art editor Andrew Shoolbred
Layout by Florrianne Henfield

Filmset and printed Offset Litho in Great Britain by
Cox & Wyman Ltd, London, Fakenham and Reading

SBN: 399–11473–4
Library of Congress Catalog Card Number: 74–19870

Contents

Introduction   7

Author's Acknowledgments   9

1 Nowhere to Somewhere 1809-42   10

2 From a View to a Check 1842-54   38

3 The Call to the Summit 1854-60   62

4 The War of Brothers 1861   86

5 Pain and Difficulty 1862   120

6 Gleams of Light 1863   150

7 Victory When It Came 1864-5   176

8 'As God gives us to see the Right'   216

Further Reading   227

Acknowledgments for Photographs   228

Index   229

Introduction

TAKEN TOGETHER, Abraham Lincoln's life and death form the perfect pattern for a national hero. From the valleys to the peaks and back to the valley – of sudden death. But once get away from the bold, simple outlines, and Lincoln's career is studded with complexities. To know him is at least to make a start in under-standing the American people during their most crucial years: the years of crisis over slavery and the Civil War.

First signs of Lincoln's heroic role appeared with his hard youth among frontiersmen and pioneers. He was enormously strong; and great height matched his strength. Caricatures were later to make him into an elongated freak. A benign freak, however, for his face though craggy was always infinitely kind. The charisma of a natural leader was his from boyhood, as was the uncanny gift for penmanship, presaging the great orator to come. But he carried the perpetual scars of his origins in an extraordinary uncouthness. While his language could rise to the sublimest heights, it retained traces of the roughest folk idiom. 'The bottom is out of the tub', he would say when the war was going badly. A general who hesitated had 'got the "slows"'. Once, when reviewing troops, his lanky legs seemed about to tangle themselves with those of his horse and bring them both down. But it was not the President's uncouthness which was to be his downfall: rather, his incomparable success, provoking mad envy and the assassin's bullet.

In telling this irresistible story – five thousand books are said to have been written about Lincoln – Lord Longford does not forget the impact upon Lincoln of his family. Especially moving are his relations with his wife Mary, whose strange case history is here brought up to date in accordance with the latest research.

The outstanding contribution, however, of Lord Longford is on the side of Lincoln's titanic public struggles, as both President and Commander-in-Chief. Lincoln had taken up a double-edged sword – emancipation of the slaves *and* preservation of the Union – a sword 'which none but he can wield', to quote Macaulay's epic *Horatius*. Even Lincoln himself could not always wield it, for the twin causes, as Lord Longford points out, often cut against one another. A former British Cabinet Minister and authority on recent

Irish history, Lord Longford is powerfully equipped to trace the complicated development of Lincoln's ideals. He does so with penetrating lucidity, having visited the Civil War battlefields and talked with American experts. The great question, as he sees it, is what would have happened if the actor John Wilkes Booth had not fired his single-shot derringer on 14 April 1865. Lord Longford says of Lincoln: 'To the end of his life he was hoping to bring about a social revolution and a reconciliation between North and South at the same time. Who can say that if he had lived he would not have succeeded?'

Either way, Lincoln's death is among the most gripping tragedies of history. Ford's Theatre where he was murdered, the tiny round hole in the door of the President's box through which Booth peeped, the folds of the Stars-and-Stripes ripped by Booth's heel as he leapt from the box on to the stage after firing, the red brick house opposite into which Lincoln was carried, the black horse-hair furnishings in the parlour where Mary wept and fainted, the little bedroom where Lincoln died – to explore these scenes of Lincoln's last night in Washington is to feel that the American Civil War is a thousand aeons away and at the same time vividly present. More than once Lord Longford finds himself returning to Lincoln's world-famous speech delivered over the dead at Gettysburg. With the change of a word or two it could be Lincoln's own epitaph: 'We here highly resolve that this man shall not have died in vain . . . that government of the people, by the people, for the people, shall not perish from the earth.'

Elizabeth Longford

Author's Acknowledgments

I am deeply grateful to Gwen Keeble, Barbara Winch and Annemarie Obolensky for their help in preparing the manuscript; to Philip Kaiser for his advice on reading; to Nancy Poland of the *Washington Post* for her help at all stages, and to her and Sherman Poland for their great kindness to my wife and myself in Washington and in escorting us to Gettysburg and some of the Virginian battlefields; to Elizabeth for her stirring companionship during the summer days while I wrote my book and she wrote hers.

Frank Longford

1 Nowhere to Somewhere 1809-42

As THE NINETEENTH CENTURY RECEDES FROM US, Abraham
Lincoln stands out ever more incontestably above all other
American statesmen. In the whole of modern political history one
cannot readily point to his superior; it is difficult even to suggest
his equal. We pay tribute to his moral grandeur, his triumphant
prosecution of noble causes and his extraordinary gift of words,
eloquent, humorous and tender.

Lincoln's permanent achievement was produced in little more
than four years. He was born in 1809, the same year as Gladstone,
his only British rival as a statesman/moralist. He was assassinated
in 1865, when Gladstone had not yet reached his zenith and had
three premierships and thirty years of parliamentary life ahead
of him. In some ways there is a closer analogy with Churchill,
another supreme war leader and orator who, like Lincoln, required
a tremendous conflagration to bring him fulfilment. But Churchill
was born in Blenheim Palace, son of a Chancellor of the Exchequer
and a society lady of high influence, Lincoln in utter poverty, of a
father who drifted downwards and a mother, probably illegitimate,

who died when he was a small boy. All statesmen of genius have certain points in common, but between Churchill and Lincoln the contrasts of personality are at least as striking as one would expect from their backgrounds.

'Abraham Lincoln's nomination for the Presidency', wrote Lord Charnwood, one of his best biographers, 'was on the whole the most surprising nomination ever made in America. Other Presidents have been born in poverty, but none ever bore the scars of poverty so plainly.' He was in fact born in a log cabin, fairly near Hodgenville, Kentucky. The cabin, we are told, was eighteen feet wide and sixteen feet long, with a dirt floor and a clay chimney to carry away the smoke. His father, Thomas Lincoln, had been born into a prosperous Virginian farming family. Thomas himself, however, was a failure in life by any ordinary standards. The stories have no doubt been exaggerated, but one authority who does his best for him, admits that 'a steady retrogression marked his later years'. Eventually he seems to have forgotten how to write his name. Lincoln, it is painful to recall, seemed to feel little filial tenderness towards him. Informed repeatedly that his father's end was near, he failed to answer, eventually explaining that he 'could write nothing which could do any good'. He sent a pious message through his stepbrother, but did not manage to attend the funeral.

Towards his mother he felt quite differently. Endless controversies have centred around her life and parentage. There seems, however, little doubt that she came into the world as Nancy Hanks and that when she was quite small, her mother married Henry Sparrow. Lincoln was convinced that she had been an illegitimate child and that her true father was an unknown Virginian planter from whom he himself had derived some of his principal qualities. He spoke about her seldom, but once burst out: 'God bless my mother. All that I am and ever hope to be, I owe to her.' She is said to have been intelligent, deeply religious, kindly and affectionate, but virtually illiterate. When she signed a legal document, she made her mark. She died when Lincoln was nine.

His father soon married Sarah Johnston of Kentucky, a widow with three children, a woman of somewhat more culture, and a friend to Lincoln at all stages of his life. Thomas Lincoln had mocked at Abe's desire for knowledge: 'I suppose', he said, 'Abe is still fooling hisself with eddication; I tried to stop it, but he had got that fool idea in his head and it can't be got out.' But his stepmother Sarah was at great pains to encourage him in his studies.

Lincoln's much-loved stepmother, Sarah Bush Johnston. (Lincoln National Life Foundation, Fort Wayne, Indiana)

13

14

Cotton Plantation by Giroux. (Courtesy Museum of Fine Arts, Boston; M. and M. Karolik Collection)

His formal schooling did not add up to more than a year, but he went on reading indomitably by himself; the Bible in the first place, then *Aesop's Fables*, *Pilgrim's Progress*, *Robinson Crusoe*, Weems's *Life of Washington* and a few other works of high quality. Lincoln attended altogether five schools, two in Kentucky, three in Indiana, none of them, it will be realized, for any length of time. One of his school-mates, at his second school, has left a description of his appearance which superficially was not attractive: 'His skin was shrivelled and yellow. His shoes, when he had any, were low. He wore buckskin breeches, linsey-woolsey shirt and a cap made of the skin of a squirrel or coon. His breeches were baggy and lacked by several inches meeting the tops of his shoes, thereby exposing his shin-bone, sharp, blue and narrow.' But Lincoln is remembered as a general favourite. He was the best speller, the

BELOW A flatboat going down the Mississippi. It was in this type of boat that Lincoln, John Hanks and John D. Johnston took a load of cargo down the Mississippi to New Orleans in 1831. It was Lincoln's second visit to the bustling port (OPPOSITE), and the horrors of slavery which he saw on these trips made a lasting impression on him. (Radio Times Hulton Picture Library)

best penman and perhaps the best all-round scholar among the boys of the neighbourhood. It would be wrong therefore to imply that he learned nothing at school.

But while all this was going on, the family moved more than once, firstly to another place in Kentucky and, when Lincoln was seven, to what is now Spencer County, Indiana. Here Lincoln recalled later, in an autobiographical note: 'Abraham, though very young, was large for his age and had an axe put into his hands at once; and from that until his twenty-third year he was almost constantly handling that most useful instrument – less of course in ploughing and harvesting seasons.' Thomas Lincoln built yet another one-room cabin, occupied at one time by as many as nine people, including Sarah Lincoln, her three children by her first marriage, and Lincoln's cousin, Dennis Hanks.

But Thomas Lincoln did not prosper in Indiana. In 1830 (when
Abraham was aged twenty-one), he sold his farm for $125 and
moved off, first to one part of Illinois and then to another. On the
second occasion, however, Lincoln broke away. He, his stepbrother John Johnston and his cousin John Hanks set off on a
cargo trip to New Orleans (their second), on behalf of a promoter
called Offutt. On their return they settled close to Offutt at the
little village of New Salem, situated above the Sangamon River.
Here they awaited whatever might befall. Lincoln described himself as having been at this time (July 1831) 'a piece of floating
driftwood'.

He was by now a giant of a man, six feet four, and enormously
strong, distinguished too in spite of his lack of schooling for his
exceptional studiousness which, in later years, he somewhat
played down. The earliest specimen of his handwriting is under-
standably crude (the lines were based, we are told, on a current
jingle):

> Abraham Lincoln his hand and pen
> he will be good but god knows When

He had revealed a talent for satirical verse and an occasional
practical joke not always appreciated by his victim. The family
of Grigsby, for example, had incurred his dislike. When two of the
Grigsby brothers made a joint wedding, Lincoln arranged matters
so that they entered the wrong beds on the wedding night. He
afterwards commemorated the event in a biblical parody.

Other legends exhibit him as a naughty boy among naughty
boys. His gift, later so famous, for concocting or repeating stories
(some of them coarse) developed early. Mr Leonard Swett, however – later Attorney-General of the United States – who came to
know him well, puts this in perspective: 'Almost any man who will
tell a very vulgar story has in a degree a vulgar mind, but it was
not so with him; with all his Puritan character and exalted morality
and sensibility, when hunting for wit he had not ability to dis-
criminate between the vulgar and refined substances from which
he extracted it.' Something of the sort seems to have been present
always. But his stepmother, after his death, could say of him:
'Abe was a good boy; he was kind to everybody and to everything,
and always accommodated others if he could.' Even in these early
days, one can detect the beginnings of the charisma and a certain
indefinable uniqueness. His friend Speed, with whom he shared a
house in Springfield a few years later, wrote of him: 'He was so

L	M	f	P
71	1	3	10
44	2	5	16
26	1	5	34
71	1	3	10

Subr

y	f	J	B
48	0	4	2
12	0	3	1
36	0	10	1
48	0	1	2

# of Land Measure

A	R	P	
	4	40	
12	1	10	
5	3	17	
6	1	33	
12	1	10	

A	R	P	
	4	40	
17	3	17	
12	3	23	
4	3	34	
17	3	17	

A	r	h	
	4	40	
28	4	4	
19	1	28	
8	3	12	
28	1	4	

# of Dry Measure

th	B	P	
	36	4	
17	2	1	
10	1	3	
7	0	2	
17	2	1	

C	C	h	
	36	4	
40	1	2	
16	5	1	
23	32	1	
40	1	2	

q	B	P	
	8	4	
19	4	1	
12	4	2	
6	1	3	
19	1	1	

Abraham Lincoln
his hand and pen
he will be good but
god knows When

Black Hawk, war leader of the Sauk and Fox tribes during the Indian War of 1832. Lincoln enlisted when the war broke out and was quickly elected captain of his company. Years later he wrote that he had 'not since had any success in life which gave him so much satisfaction'. (Illinois State Historical Library)

unlike all the men that I had ever known before or known since, that there is no one with whom I can compare him.'

Lincoln began as a clerk at $15 a month in Offutt's store and soon won local prominence as a wrestling champion. Jack Armstrong, leader of the roughest crowd in the neighbourhood, challenged him to a wrestling match in which Lincoln proved himself the better man, though accounts of the outcome vary. Lincoln was welcomed into the group and made their leader. Soon he was coming to the front in the New Salem debating society and

20

in next to no time (still only twenty-three) he was putting himself forward as a candidate for the Illinois state legislature.

Now arose a savage but brief war with the Indians who still roamed through the trackless woods and prairies of northern Illinois, too close to New Salem for comfort. Lincoln volunteered for service; was elected captain of a company, as always a popular choice, and served altogether for about eighty days – an experience he ridiculed afterwards. In a speech in Congress, when his opponents were magnifying the military record of their candidate, Lewis Cass, for President, he poked this kind of fun: 'By the way, Mr Speaker, did you know that I am a military hero? Yes, Sir! In the days of the Black Hawk war. I fought, bled and came away. . . . It is quite certain I did not break my sword, for I had none to break, but I bent a musket pretty badly on one occasion.' 'If', he said, 'Cass saw any live fighting Indians, it was more than I did, but I had a good many bloody struggles with the mosquitoes. . . .'

He arrived back just in time for the election. This he lost, running eighth among thirteen candidates – the only time, he would recall, that he was defeated in a direct vote of the people. Although he was more or less a newcomer to New Salem, he received 277 votes out of the 304 in his own neighbourhood. His election address exhibited some of that personal poignancy so familiar later: 'I am young and unknown to many of you. I was born and have ever remained in the most humble walks of life. . . . If the good people in their wisdom see fit to keep me in the background, I have been too familiar with disappointments to be very much chagrined.' Now and always, we are assured by Herndon, for many years his partner, Lincoln was immensely ambitious. This may well be true until the fires of the Civil War burned ambition out of his soul. But from his earliest moments in politics, he well understood the appeal of the modest demeanour.

Lincoln lived at New Salem altogether for six years. During that time he read Shakespeare and Burns, studied mathematics and learned many lessons about life in a hard school. The visible balance sheet when he left in 1837 was somewhat mixed. Financially he was no better off than when he arrived. Indeed, worse off on paper. Offutt's store had soon faded out and he and a friend tried store-keeping on their own, with unhappy consequences. His partner died. Lincoln manfully shouldered the whole debt of some $1,100, but could not pay it off until long after he had left New Salem.

At one moment he had thought of becoming a blacksmith, where his great strength would have given him an advantage, but saw no future in it. In May 1833 he became the New Salem Postmaster, at a salary of $155 a year, with one or two perquisites. He used to carry the letters around in his hat, acquiring a habit which he made famous on higher levels later. He supplemented his small income by splitting rails, working as a farm hand, helping at the mill and assisting a local newspaper. Then, as always, he was utterly devoid of false pride and pomposity. He became a Deputy Surveyor for the county, but the load of debts still hung over him.

The year 1834 saw him elected, at the age of twenty-five, as a Whig member of the Illinois legislature. The campaign had thrown him into contact with John T. Stuart, the Whig leader for the county, who formed a high opinion of him and advised him to study law. Lincoln had always been interested in the subject but had hitherto lacked the confidence to pursue it. Now he threw himself into the task of becoming a lawyer. Stuart's partner recalls Lincoln coming to their office to borrow books: 'He was the most uncouth looking young man I ever saw. He seemed to have but little to say; seemed to feel timid, with a tinge of sadness visible in his countenance, but when he did talk all this disappeared for the time and he demonstrated that he was both strong and acute. He surprised us more and more at every visit.' Why these repeated references to his uncouthness? Poverty does not necessarily leave such an imprint. Nor genius, if it comes to that. Nor exceptional height. But there is no doubt that such an impression clung to Lincoln and handicapped him till his election as President and afterwards.

His party was all the time a minority in the Illinois Assembly. The Democratic majority took pride in the slogan 'All Whigs ought to be whipped out of office like dogs out of a meat-house.' But Lincoln was the last man to be brow-beaten. He played a large part in bringing the capital from Vandalia in 1839 to Springfield. By this time he was the floor leader of the Whigs and his reputation was spreading rapidly. He was now thirty years of age.

His relations with women over the same period had been unfortunate in two well-known instances. In the one case, the extent of the tragedy is vehemently disputed; in the other he emerged unscathed, if less than heroically. The legend of Lincoln's romance with Ann Rutledge has passed into the folklore of America. In 1890 what was thought to be her body was removed from its resting-place and re-interred in a cemetery more accessible to visitors. Her new tombstone carried a poem by Edgar Lee Masters, which ended with the words:

I am Ann Rutledge who sleep beneath these weeds,
Beloved of Abraham Lincoln,
Wedded to him, not through union,
But through separation.
Bloom forever, O Republic,
From the dust of my bosom.

Most authorities on Lincoln are very sceptical about the whole business, yet a minimum substratum of fact is indisputable. There certainly was a pretty girl of twenty-two called Ann Rutledge, apparently with blue eyes and auburn hair. Lincoln certainly lodged in her father's tavern when he first came to New Salem; she did undoubtedly die of a mysterious disease which baffled the doctors. And even those who on the whole pooh-pooh the legend accept the fact Lincoln took her death unusually hard.

In its more dramatic version Ann was engaged to a young man called McNamar who, having made a small fortune, returned to New York to assist his family. Various accidents, including illness, delayed his return. Nothing was heard from him. Ann felt that her promise to him had lapsed and Lincoln felt himself free to win her hand. She accepted his proposal of marriage but, according to the story, Ann now found herself in an appalling condition of mental conflict – torn between her two fiancés. She was unable to eat or sleep and soon went down with fever. According to Herndon, his future partner, Lincoln visited her sick-room and found her emaciated and dying. 'The meeting was quite as much as either could bear', asserted Herndon, 'and more than Lincoln could endure. The voice, the face, the features of her; the love, sympathy and interview fastened themselves on his heart and soul for ever.' On 25 August 1835 Ann died.

Lincoln's mind, it is said, became seriously deranged. 'The effect', recalled one of Ann's brothers, 'upon Mr Lincoln's mind was terrible. He became plunged in despair and many of his friends feared that reason would desert her throne. His extraordinary emotions were regarded as strong evidence of the existence of the tenderest relations between himself and the deceased.' With the help of devoted friends, Lincoln gradually recovered, but it is claimed that he never loved anyone so much again and that 'His heart was buried in the grave with Ann Rutledge.'

Nothing of all this was known to the general public for many years. Hence the later scepticism. An article along these lines appeared in 1862, it is true, but it did not attract much attention.

The indefatigable Herndon, however, got to work thereafter and collected a large supply of information, much of it contradictory. He achieved a massive impact with a celebrated lecture in 1866 and developed the theme with gusto in his reminiscences. The full truth will always remain a matter of speculation. It seems certain, however, that Lincoln was at the least immensely fond of Ann Rutledge and possible that he wished to marry her. Whether or not he was deranged by her death, he was for the time being deeply stricken.

His next romance was with Mary Owens, who first appeared in New Salem in 1833, but then not again until 1836, by which time Lincoln was recovering from the death of Ann. A man who saw her at the time wrote ecstatically: 'She was tall, portly, had large blue eyes and the finest trimmings I ever saw.' She was jovial, social and entertaining, had a liberal English education and was considered wealthy. Lincoln became, it seems, infatuated with her, but in a year it was all over. Soon after he moved to Springfield in 1837, he 'wriggled out', to use Benjamin Thomas's phrase, of his entanglement. In his final letter, whose subtlety and ambiguity Mr Gladstone could hardly have improved on, he enabled her to break off relations without loss of dignity. One remark of hers about Lincoln has gone down to history: 'I thought him deficient in those little links which make up the chain of a woman's happiness – at least it was so in my case.' But speaking of Lincoln shortly before her death, she referred to him as 'a man with a heart full of human kindness and a head full of commonsense'.

We must return for a moment to Lincoln's entry in 1837 into Springfield, still a small town with, at that time, some fifteen hundred inhabitants, but for a young politician the coming place. Joshua Speed, a successful merchant, later Lincoln's most intimate friend, has left a vivid account of their first meeting. Lincoln, who had ridden into town on a borrowed horse, came into the store, set his saddlebags on the counter and enquired 'what the furniture for a single bedstead would cost?' Speed figured that it would come to $17, to which Lincoln answered: 'It is probably cheap enough; but I want to say that, cheap as it is, I have not the money to pay. But if you will credit me until Christmas, and my experiment here as a lawyer is a success, I will pay you then. If I fail in that I will probably never pay you at all.' Speed was struck by the tone of the stranger's voice and 'his gloomy and melancholy face'. He felt moved by pity for him and suggested a plan to enable him to achieve his purpose without incurring any debt. 'I have a very

24

large room', he said, 'and a very large double bed in it, which you
are perfectly welcome to share with me, if you choose.' 'Where is
your room?' asked Lincoln. 'Upstairs', said Speed, pointing the
way. Without saying anything more, the stranger took his saddlebags on his arm, went upstairs, set them down on the floor, came
down again and with a beaming face, all pleasure and smiles,
exclaimed: 'Well, Speed, I am moved.' It is a delightful and significant story. One is struck by the sheer poverty of Lincoln at a time
when he was already making his name as a member of the state
legislature, by references to his melancholy aspect, so often
referred to in other chronicles, and by the irresistible, the almost
seductive charm.

As we have already seen, the political leader Stuart encouraged

25

S. T. LOGAN & E. D. BAKER,
ATTORNEYS AND COUNSELLORS AT LAW.
WILL practice, in conjunction, in the Cir-
Courts of this Judicial District, and n the Circuit
Courts of the Counties of Pike, Schuyler and Peoria.
Springfield, march, 1887.   81-t

J. T. STUART AND A. LINCOLN.
ATTORNEYS and Counsellors at Law, will practice,
conjointly, in the Courts of this Judicial Circuit.—
Office No. 4 Hoffman's Row, up stairs.
Springfield, april 12, 1837.   4

THE partnership heretofore existing between the un-
dersigned, has been dissolved by mutual consent.—
The business will be found in the hands of John T. Stuart.
                                   JOHN T. STUART,
April 12, 1837.   84   HENRY E. DUMMER.

him to read law, and later took him into partnership. It is convenient to mention here that Lincoln practised law with him until
1841; then until 1844 with Stephen T. Logan, the undisputed head
of the local Bar. In December 1844, he opened his own office and
took into partnership young William H. Herndon, nine years
younger than Lincoln, and therefore twenty-six at the time.
Herndon, son of a former colleague of Lincoln in the legislature,
met Lincoln while he was working in Speed's store and had been
encouraged by him to study law. His reminiscences, published in
1889, not to mention various lectures and much information
supplied to others, make sure that his name will crop up repeatedly
in any biography of Lincoln. No one who reads his memoirs can
doubt that he was an entertaining colleague with an acute mind,
though with doubtful judgment and a considerable power of
fantasy. Although devoid of social aspirations and lacking in
social graces, Lincoln moved in Springfield's most respected
circles, while Herndon, by reason of his misadventures (for
example, he frequently got drunk) 'never made the social grade'
(Thomas). Be all that as it may, the partnership operated actively
and harmoniously for sixteen years, indeed until Lincoln became
President.

Every historian has drawn considerably on Herndon, but most
of them hold him guilty of serious inaccuracies and no little fiction.
The account he gives of the events leading to Lincoln's marriage

26

is a case in point. When Herndon first met Mary Todd at a ball, he became so fascinated by her pliant grace that he likened her to a serpent. According to Herndon, Mrs Lincoln as she became took the intended compliment as an insult and never forgave him. Whether or not that story is true, Herndon was so biased against her that modern scholars are agreed in treating his picture of her with a good deal of disdain.

Much has been written about Mary Lincoln in the last few years. Two plays about her have been produced. In 1972 a most impressive volume appeared, *Mary Todd Lincoln – Her Life and Letters*, by the well-known authority on Lincoln, Justin Turner, and his daughter-in-law Linda Levitt Turner, with an introduction by Fawn M. Brodie. More than six hundred letters of Mary Lincoln survive. All the available letters are published in this collection, most of them deriving from the seventeen years after her husband's death, but many of them written while they were still together. The Herndon picture disappears. Psychological controversies will always remain, but the external facts are fairly certain.

Mary Todd was a sister of Mrs Edwards, whose husband had been Attorney-General of Illinois and was a colleague of Lincoln's in the legislature. She was herself a leader of the smartest set in Springfield. They were a lively group who called themselves 'The Coterie', and were called by those who were not admitted 'The Edwards Clique'. Mary Todd's great-grandfather had been one of the revolutionary generals. To quote Justin and Linda Turner: 'The family in its various branches – Todds, Porters, Parkers – boasted Revolutionary War heroes and Indian fighters, successful farmers and merchants, politicians and philanthropists. Wherever they settled, they seemed to thrive. They married and intermarried, held on to their money, led useful lives and considered themselves aristocrats.' Her father, of Lexington, Kentucky, was a state senator, a business man of considerable wealth and social position, the president of a bank and an owner of slaves.

She had been educated at exclusive schools, where she learned French which she spoke fluently, music, dancing and other graces. She would seem to have been even fuller of life and attraction than Mary Owens, though not perhaps as beautiful. Like her predecessor, she tended to plumpness (130 lbs against 150, but she was a good deal shorter; she was in fact five feet two inches). She had a small, upturned nose, a broad forehead, a rosy complexion and soft brown hair. Her chin was rather prominent and her mouth rather thin; the pictures make her look rather tight-lipped and stern, but in real life her eyes were merry and kind and she smiled often. We are told that her figure was 'rounded, buxom and ideally suited to the fashions of the day', that her arms and hands were exquisitely shaped and that her gestures were quick and graceful. She was witty and warm-hearted, but highly strung; imperious and demanding and capable of sudden rages – 'the very creature of excitement'. She was the antithesis but also, as it proved, the complement of Lincoln, with his insistent strain of sadness and his slowly burning fires.

Springfield gave a grand cotillion ball in December 1839, in honour of the arrival of the legislature. Mary Todd was a belle. She noticed a group of men in the corner of the room laughing and talking, but not dancing. Her cousin, Major John Stuart, told her that in the centre of the group was his partner, Abraham Lincoln, who did not dance much, but was a great teller of stories, which some of the young men liked listening to more than dancing. Lincoln was soon captivated as completely as by Mary Owens, and got cold feet just as quickly. At one moment he and Mary Todd are found reading poetry together and discussing politics. We are told that it was usually Mary who led the conversation. 'Mr Lincoln would sit at her side and listen. He scarcely said a word, but gazed on her as if irresistibly drawn towards her by a superior and unseen power.' By December 1840 she and Abraham Lincoln had reached an understanding and were talking openly of marriage.

Yet on New Year's Day 1841, a date referred to later by Lincoln as 'the fatal first of January', suddenly for the time being the whole thing broke down and the engagement came to an end. They parted, it was supposed, for ever. Herndon tells a tale of the wedding being arranged for that date, of everything being ready to begin, but of Lincoln failing to turn up and Mary being jilted in the sight of all. This version is now rejected by everyone. We can discard along with it, somewhat contemptuously, Herndon's theory that Mary lost at that moment any love she might have felt for Lincoln and pursued him thereafter out of a mixture of ambition and revenge. Two factors are offered by the genuine experts as probably combining to precipitate the break-up and the eighteen months' estrangement that followed: first, Lincoln's extreme sensitivity; secondly, the firm opposition of Mary Todd's family, which can today be put down to snobbery, but in those days, in all the circumstances, was not unnatural. As Lincoln wrote earlier to Mary Owens: 'I am afraid you would not be satisfied. There is a great deal of flourishing in carriages here which it would be your doom to see without sharing in it. You would have to be poor without the means of hiding your poverty.' The same considerations applied still more in the case of Mary Todd, who indeed was to pass through this precise experience. Mary Todd bore her distress with dignity. She wrote to a friend that he 'deems me unworthy of notice, as I have not met him in the gay world for months. With the usual comfort of misery, I imagine that others were as seldom gladdened by his presence as my humble self, yet I would that the case were different, that he would once more resume his Station in Society, that "Richard should be himself again", much, much happiness would it afford me.' Lincoln was shattered, no doubt torn by every kind of self-doubt and self-criticism. Speed helped to nurse him back to health on his farm in Kentucky.

Speed was encountering problems of precisely the same kind in his own life. Lincoln was full of sensitive understanding and much more practical than in dealing with his own situation. Speed had no doubt later on about the effects of his own happy marriage on Lincoln. 'One thing is plainly discernible: if I had not been married happily, far more happily than I ever expected to be, he would not have married.'

Lincoln's friend and physician Dr Anson G. Henry took a hand. So did Simeon Francis, editor of Springfield's Whig newspaper, the *Sangamo Journal*. He engineered a surprise meeting for the couple at his home. Mary and Lincoln arrived separately, neither expecting to meet the other. In the Turners' phrase, they were 'shyly delighted when Mrs Francis urged, "Be friends"'. Secret meetings followed at Francis's home. The engagement was revived and on 4 November 1842, they were married by the Episcopal minister in the house of the Edwards who were won over by the inevitable. About thirty relatives and friends were present. The words Lincoln had had engraved on Mary's wedding ring were 'Love Is Eternal'. The marriage, as the Turners put it, was 'a triumph of love over the odds and that love would survive everything including death'.

There were plenty of trials in front of them. Lincoln was not everyone's idea of a perfect husband. Mary, to quote Herbert Agar, was 'a gently reared woman, married to one of the most untidy, careless, unconventional and moody of men. Although it is a virtue to think deeply, prolonged and impenetrable silences in the home do not make for marriage ease.' He was completely irregular in all his habits, with no fixed time for eating and no

THE PEOPLE OF THE STATE OF ILLINOIS.

To any Minister of the Gospel, or other authorised Person—GREETING.

THESE are to Licence and permit you to join in the holy bands of Matrimony *Abraham Lincoln* and *Mary Todd* of the County of Sangamon and State of Illinois, and for so doing, this shall be your sufficient warrant.

Given under my hand and seal of office, at Springfield, in said County this 4th day of November 1842

N. W. Matheny Clerk.

Solemnized on the same 4th day of Nov. 1842 *Charles Dresser*

fixed time for going to bed nor for getting up. His wife's sense of social dignity in keeping with her family's excellent position in Kentucky did not appeal to him. Asked about the spelling of her family name, he replied: 'One "d" is enough for God, but the Todds need two.' This could be taken in good part or otherwise.

Always she believed in his destiny and the career that would lead to it, but it was the man, not the career, she loved. They started married life on a much lower standard than she was accustomed to. Before her marriage she had been used to a good many servants and spacious living. She and Lincoln now settled in a place called the *Globe Tavern*, where they took two rooms. When their son Robert was born, in August 1843, they still could not afford a nurse. In 1844, they were able to buy a home of their own, but Mary Lincoln not only had to do all the cooking, she had to sew, mend and launder all the clothes. During her time as President's wife, she was appallingly extravagant, entertaining and dressing herself far more lavishly than her allowance made possible. No doubt the restricted circumstances of her early married life built up a repressed desire to throw restraint to the winds, if ever the chance came her way. No doubt there was also a deeper psychological problem. As a child she exhibited an obsessional hunger

for elegant clothes. At ten she and a young friend had tried to fashion hoops to go under their skirts. As time went on, she revealed extreme symptoms at the same time of extravagance and of miserliness in the sense that she imagined herself on the point of ruin. But as Dr Evans in his psychological study has written: 'This complex mania for money, extravagance and miserliness, is well-known to psychiatrists. It is present in many people who are accepted as normal.' The one area in which she was demonstrably irrational was that of finance, but the Turners point out that in many of her letters she shows plenty of good sense even here.

Unfortunately, of all the letters that passed between Mary Lincoln and her husband, only three survive. But one, written after he had known her for more than seven years, is perhaps significant: 'You are entirely free from headache? That is good, considering it is the first Spring you have been free from it since we were acquainted.' One likes to believe that today her nervous troubles would have been diagnosed earlier and coped with better.

Four sons were born between 1843 and 1853. Robert Todd lived long and usefully, but left behind him only daughters; Eddie died when he was four; Willie died in 1862 during the Civil War. Lincoln was heart-broken and his wife's mental balance, always delicately poised, was seriously shaken. Thomas ('Tad') died a few years after Lincoln. No parents were more devoted than the Lincolns. Willie and Tad were adored and may be said to have been spoiled by both of them.

Mary Lincoln lived for seventeen years after Lincoln's death. The whole period of her widowhood was tragic, redeemed only by her memories of Lincoln – above all by their last drive together, with their plans for the future – and by her strong religious faith. She wandered about the world like a lost soul, plagued with debts from her former extravagance, most ungenerously treated by Congress and seeking to obtain financial help by humiliating activities. She was confined near the end for a year in a mental home, but finished her life at the age of sixty-four in the Springfield house of her sister, Mrs Edwards, where she had first met Lincoln. She had spent the months there in a darkened room, lying on one side of the bed so as not to 'disturb' the President's place beside her. To quote the Turners once more: 'Unlike many married couples of the day, these two had consciously chosen each other for reasons that made their life together continuously rewarding.' There was mutual respect, shared interests and 'a physical passion that never diminished'.

ABOVE The Lincolns' home in
Springfield. They bought the house
in 1844 and lived there until they
moved to Washington in 1861.
(Illinois State Historical Library)

OPPOSITE ABOVE The sitting-room
and (BELOW) the front parlour of
the house. (Illinois State Historical
Society)

Senator Sumner had never flagged in his efforts to obtain for her a reasonable pension. In 1870, after a bitter struggle, he carried through the Senate a reduced measure to this effect by twenty-eight votes to twenty. (It was supplemented later on.) With tears in his eyes, he said:

> Surely the honourable members of the Senate must be weary of casting mud on the garments of the wife of Lincoln; those same garments on which one terrible night, five years ago, gushed out the blood and brains of Abraham Lincoln. She sat beside him in the theatre and she received that pitiful, that holy deluge on her hands and skirts, because she was the chosen companion of his heart. She loved him. I speak of that which I know. He had all her love. And Lincoln loved, as only his mighty heart could love, Mary Lincoln.

This was true in itself, and is for our purposes a large part of the truth.

In the months before Lincoln married, there occurred two incidents which did him no good at the time. Early in 1842, he gave an address on temperance, a subject on which he was well-qualified to speak, having been since early days a strict teetotaller. His speech included this sensational observation: 'If we take habitual drunkards as a class, their heads and their hearts will bear an advantageous comparison with those of any other class.' Herndon was at the door of the church as the people passed out and, not surprisingly perhaps, the comments were most unfavourable. 'It is a shame', said one man, 'that he should be permitted to abuse us in the house of the Lord.' That seemed to be the general opinion.

A second episode brought him to the very edge of a duel, although he was strongly opposed to duelling both then and later. A certain James Shields, a gallant, hot-headed Irishman, the state auditor, had refused on behalf of the state to accept the much-depreciated state money at its face value in payment of taxes. The Opposition Party, the Whigs, turned their guns on him. Lincoln through his influence over the *Springfield Journal*, had excellent opportunities for mischief. Encouraged by his friend Mary Todd, he wrote an article purporting to come from a poor widow, 'Rebecca', gravely damaged by Shields's decision. The article was very long, very ponderous and very offensive. Shields, not unnaturally furious, discovered that the author was Lincoln and challenged him to a duel. Lincoln reluctantly but firmly accepted Shield's challenge but, having choice of weapons, opted for cavalry broadsides of the largest size. These were to be wielded across a plank set edgewise in the ground, neither man being allowed to retreat more than eight feet from the plank. Lincoln, with his immensely long arms, was giving himself an overwhelming advantage, probably in the desire to get the whole thing laughed out of court. Duelling was forbidden in Illinois, so all concerned made their way across the Mississippi to the appointed spot. But just in time, the seconds discovered a way out. An agreed statement announced that 'all papers in relation to the matter in controversy had been withdrawn', so that Lincoln could not be accused of having negotiated under threats. Lincoln said afterwards to Herndon this only: 'I did not intend to hurt Shields, unless I did so clearly in self-defence. If it had been necessary, I could have split him from the crown of his head to the end of his backbone.' On the whole, he seems to have been ashamed of the episode, perhaps most of all because of the unworthy satire in which it started. With his astonishing range of anecdote, mimicry and wisecracks, it must have been difficult for him to refrain from turning his gift of ridicule on individuals, but from this time onwards he seems to have made great efforts to keep it in check.

2 From a View to a Check 1842-54

THERE ARE NO EASY DIVIDING LINES in Lincoln's career between 1832, when he first stood for the Illinois legislature, aged twenty-three, and 1849, when he finished his two years in the United States Congress convinced (aged forty) that his political career was at an end. The main dates, however, are easy to pick out: 1834, elected to Illinois legislature; 1836, qualifies as a lawyer; 1837, moves to Springfield; 1842, marries; 1846, elected to Congress; 1847, takes his seat there.

It seems convenient here to indicate his political attitudes up to 1849 and his showing as a lawyer in these years and in those which followed, when he 'rode the circuit' most actively. Lincoln's life was eventually dominated by – and he himself did more than any- one to dominate – the settlement of the slavery issue all over America. But in the years 1832-49 we hear no more than the rumblings of the coming storm. When Lincoln stood unsuccess- fully for the Illinois legislature for the first time in 1832, he told the electorate: 'My politics are short and sweet, like the old woman's dance. I am in favour of a National Bank. I am in favour of the internal improvement system and high protective tariffs. These are my sentiments and political principles.' He had identified himself as a follower of Henry Clay and as a Whig and, by and large, what he said then he stood by later.

A few words are necessary about the Party situation as it was and as it developed. The labels are, admittedly, confusing. It is claimed for the Democratic Party, founded by Thomas Jefferson, that it is 'the oldest continuously existing political instrumentality in the United States'. The same authority, however, points out that it was not until Andrew Jackson – the great populist President – was elected in 1828 that it changed its name from Republican to Democratic. For some years previously, since the collapse of the Federalist Party, the Republicans had been left without organized opposition. They contained, however, a number of conflicting groups. Each followed some outstanding leader such as Henry Clay or Andrew Jackson.

About the same time as the Jacksonian Republicans became Democrats, the Clay Republicans acquired a separate identity as National Republicans. By 1834 they became known as Whigs and continued as such till 1854 when they fell apart on the slavery issue and disappeared from the scene. (They were succeeded in the North by the new Republican Party.) During Lincoln's active career until 1854, the two main parties were the Whigs, to which he belonged, and the Democrats, who were usually in office.

PREVIOUS PAGES The earliest known photograph of Lincoln, made from a daguerrotype. It was probably taken in Springfield in 1846. (Library of Congress)

40

The name Whig associated that Party with antagonism to executive encroachments; certainly the Whigs under Clay's leadership were opposed to the autocratic Presidency of Andrew Jackson. In spite of that, they were the positive constructive Party. Herbert Agar is convinced that the strongest reason leading Lincoln to follow Clay so devoutly was that 'Clay devoted his life to Union-saving and for this reason Lincoln loved him.' Certainly Clay and the Whigs stood consistently and unequivocally for the Union, but on this issue there was no contradication between them and Jackson, the Democratic President from the frontier. Tariffs were naturally much more attractive to the industrialized Northern states than to the slave-owning cotton-producing South, which depended on ample foreign markets and the cheapest possible imports. In the 1830s, South Carolina showed a tendency to secession. A compromise was reached which kept the tariffs fairly low but President Jackson made it plain that secession would be prevented by force if necessary. The great Whig orator Daniel Webster coined the never-to-be-forgotten 'Liberal and Union now and forever, one and inseparable!' But Jackson was just as uncompromising and hardly less eloquent. As compared, however, with the Democrats, the Whigs laid less stress on States' Rights and a greater one on Federal responsibilities.

It will be noticed that Lincoln, in his first public manifesto, said nothing about slavery; there was no reason at that precise moment why he should. Yet by this time slavery was much more firmly established in the Southern states than it had been in the days of the Founding Fathers. The greatest of them had condemned the principle. Washington in his will provided for the emancipation of his own slaves. He told Jefferson that 'it was among his first wishes to see some plan adopted by which slavery might be abolished by law'. 'I tremble', said Jefferson, 'for my country when I reflect that God is just.'

The invention of the cotton gin had revolutionized the economic position. In 1794, the year when the gin was patented, the Southern states of America produced about two million pounds of cotton; in 1826, the South, including the new states of the south-west, produced 330 million pounds. By the time Lincoln entered politics, the figure had expanded by a further fifty per cent. Slavery was no longer looked on as a transitional experiment, but as the very life-blood of the Southern economy and its social existence. Moral rationalization was easily developed to justify its continuance and extension. Meanwhile, the industrialization

North and South

During the nineteenth century the North and South developed along increasingly divergent paths. In the North the population and industry were rapidly expanding, while in the South the economy became more and more dependent on the cotton industry, which was based on the institution of slavery.

RIGHT ABOVE Colt weapon factory in Hartford, Connecticut. (Library of Congress)
RIGHT BELOW Detail of *The Lackawanna Valley*, a romanticized Northern industrial scene painted by George Inness. (National Gallery of Art, Washington D.C.; Gift of Mrs Huttleston Rogers)

ABOVE Cotton picking on a Southern plantation. (British Museum)

LEFT A painting of Charleston, South Carolina, in the 1830s by S. Bernard. (Yale University Art Gallery, The Mabel Brady Garvan Collection)

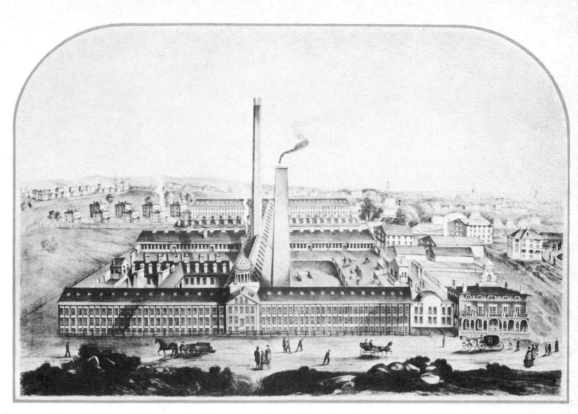

Westward the Course of Empire by Emanuel Leutze. The slavery issue was brought to a head by the question of whether or not slavery should be extended to the newly opened up territories in the West. (Thomas Gilcrease Institute of American History of Art)

of the North went forward apace in sharper and sharper contrast. Nevertheless, it was hoped that under the Missouri Compromise of 1820 slavery had been taken out of politics. That hope seems vain enough now, but in 1832 it was possible to avert one's eyes from 'the coming fury'. Under the 1820 Compromise it was agreed that slavery should be restricted to territories (areas in process of being occupied) on a line which extrapolated the southern border of Missouri. It is easy and pointless to observe that if this Compromise could have been maintained indefinitely the Civil War could have been averted. The hypothesis can now be seen to be quite unreal.

The acquisition of Louisiana in 1803 and the remorseless drive of the American people, including the new immigrants, towards the West, made a new settlement inevitable between the industrialized system of the North and the slave-holding plantations of the

44

South. The South were convinced – and who shall say that they were wrong? – that their system could not survive unless they were allowed to extend it into the new areas. There was an economic case for that belief. There was a political case for insisting that they must be allowed to increase the number of slave states *pari passu* with the free ones, if their interests were to be adequately protected. The strengthening and extension of slavery aroused passionate moral opposition among abolitionists, who demanded total abolition of slavery. William Lloyd Garrison and many others faced intense hostility, indeed persecution, for this cause. *Uncle Tom's Cabin*, one of the most powerful propagandist books ever written, was not, however, published until 1852. For a long time to come, the inevitability of the final confrontation was veiled from Lincoln and his contemporaries.

His significant utterances on slavery in the subsequent twenty years can be indicated briefly. They did not much affect his career, though the first of them was bold and even hazardous. In 1837 the Illinois legislature passed resolutions condemning the agitation of the abolitionists and declaring the constitutional powerlessness of Congress to interfere with slavery in the Southern states. Lincoln was no friend to the abolitionists; yet he, still only twenty-eight, drew up and placed on the records of the House his emphatic protests. He deprecates the promulgation of abolition documents, but he does so because 'it tends rather to increase than abate the evils of slavery'. He insists that 'The institution of slavery is founded both in justice and bad policy.' The only colleague who could be persuaded to join him in this protest was not seeking re-election.

At this early stage, therefore, he was ready (for all the 'inordinate ambition' with which he has been widely credited) to take up, at the crunch, an unpopular stand on principle. In this single term in the House of Representatives (1847–9) Lincoln was not called upon to face the slavery question urgently. But he had already written in 1844 'that it was the paramount duty of us in the free States, due to the Union of the States and perhaps to liberty itself (paradox though it may seem), to let the slavery of the other States alone. While, on the other hand, I hold it to be equally clear that we should never knowingly lend ourselves, directly or indirectly, to prevent that slavery from dying a natural death – to find new places for it to live in when it can no longer exist in the old.' This was essentially a middle position between the abolitionists and the Southern 'fire eaters'. He never shifted from this position, in

45

spite of plentiful criticism from both wings, until nearly thirty years later in the Civil War.

Even the shortest account of Lincoln's long-term attitude should include a reference to his desire for voluntary emancipation, with a cash bonus to the dispossessed slave-owners. During his last year in Congress he offered a proposal to abolish slavery in the district of Columbia, with compensation to the slave-owners, twice voting against bills which would have adopted more radical methods to achieve the same purpose. He several times, though not as often as he imagined afterwards, supported the Wilmot Proviso which would have prohibited slavery in all territory acquired from Mexico. In other words, he was resolute for moderation on this issue, but it did not occupy a large part of his attention.

Lincoln aspired to enter Congress from 1842 onwards, but did not achieve his ambition until 1846. There is one feature of his election campaign in that year which must be touched on. Lincoln was opposed by the great Revivalist preacher Peter Cartwright, who helped to encourage the impression that Lincoln had been an 'avowed infidel' while living at New Salem a few years earlier and had even written a book attacking the Bible. In later years Cartwright came to the conclusion that the story was completely false and bitterly regretted any part he had played in giving it circulation. Nevertheless, allegations of the same kind dogged Lincoln during his life and for many years after his death.

A very clear statement, signed by Lincoln, appeared in the *Illinois Gazette* of 15 August 1846. It was mainly concerned not with his beliefs but with the allegation that he was an 'open scoffer at Christianity'. Lincoln indignantly repudiated the charge that he had ever spoken 'with intentional disrespect of religion in general, or of any denominations of Christians in particular'. 'It is true', he said, 'that in early life I was inclined to believe in what I understand is called the doctrine of necessity . . . the habit of arguing thus, however, I have entirely left off for more than five years.' And he goes on to say this: 'I do not think I could myself be brought to support a man for office whom I know to be an open enemy of, and scoffer at religion.' As regards his own convictions, he is guarded. He said only: 'I am not a member of any Christian church, it is true, but I have never denied the truth of the Scriptures.' Which could presumably mean much or little.

Much clearer indications came later. In 1850 the Lincolns lost their four-year-old son Eddie. Mary Lincoln seemed unable to stop weeping; only Lincoln could persuade her to eat anything at all. To comfort her, he began attending with her the first Presbyterian Church in Springfield. Lincoln and Mary both entertained a deep respect for Doctor Smith, the pastor. Lincoln read with interest his book *The Christian's Defense*, a reply to scepticism. From that time until they went to live in Washington in 1861, they rented a pew in his church.

This period of Lincoln's life, 1832-49, ended in relative failure. He returned to Illinois as a respected member of the minority Whig Party, a statewide figure although still unknown nationally. But there seems no doubt that he was in fact thoroughly disheartened by the absence of any desire in his own area to send him back to Washington for another term, and almost as much by his total lack of influence in the control of federal patronage in Illinois. In the Illinois Assembly he had been so outstanding that his lack of distinction in the wider arena remains somewhat mysterious. His domestic programme outlined originally in his 1832 address fitted in well with the social philosophy of the Whigs – no fundamental disturbance of the economic system, but active federal intervention to help the states. He might have seemed destined to come right to the front before he was much older, but it did not turn out like that at all. One is bound to feel that he got off on the wrong foot in Congress.

Lincoln arrived in Washington at the end of 1847. In May 1846 the Congress of the United States had declared war on Mexico and although the war had not yet ended, victory was more or less complete. There was no doubt that the United States would soon annexe territory which includes the present states of California, Nevada, Utah, Arizona, New Mexico and parts of Colorado and Wyoming. The Whigs as a whole played an unhappy part in the resulting controversies. They sought to demonstrate their patriotism by voting supplies, but at the same time to place the war-guilt on the President and his administration generally. Lincoln went further than most and perhaps caused special resentment as a newcomer to national politics. President Polk insisted in his message that it was Mexico that had caused the war by shedding the blood of American citizens on American soil. One of Lincoln's colleagues from Illinois, a militant Government supporter, introduced a resolution declaring the war to be just and necessary, and demanding that an indemnity be extracted from Mexico in proportion to their obstinacy in prolonging the war. Lincoln joined his Whig colleagues in voting the resolution down, but that did not content

135,000 SETS, 270,000 VOLUMES SOLD.

UNCLE TOM'S CABIN

FOR SALE HERE.

AN EDITION FOR THE MILLION, COMPLETE IN 1 Vol., PRICE 37 1-2 CENTS.
"   "   IN GERMAN, IN 1 Vol., PRICE 50 CENTS.
"   "   IN 2 Vols., CLOTH, 6 PLATES, PRICE $1.50.
SUPERB ILLUSTRATED EDITION, IN 1 Vol., WITH 153 ENGRAVINGS,
PRICES FROM $2.50 TO $5.00.

The Greatest Book of the Age.

Slavery

Slavery was profoundly interwoven into the economy and culture of the Southern states. For long the institution had remained unquestioned, and upon such foundations had the whole life of the Southern states been erected.

OPPOSITE Negro auction room in Atlanta, Georgia. (Library of Congress)

BELOW Sale of estates, paintings and slaves in the Rotunda at New Orleans. (British Museum)

LEFT Advertisement for Harriet Beecher Stowe's book *Uncle Tom's Cabin*. First published in 1852, the book was an emotional indictment of slavery which sold in its millions in America and round the world. (Courtesy of the New-York Historical Society)

The Old House of Representatives by Samuel F. B. Morse. The hall was used by Congress until 1857 when it was vacated for newer premises. (In the Collection of the Corcoran Gallery of Art)

51

him. For a new member he took a surprisingly audacious initiative. He introduced a series of resolutions seeking to force the President to admit that Mexico and not the United States had jurisdiction over the 'Spot' where the first blood was shed. In other words, that the United States and not Mexico was the aggressor. He followed up his resolutions by remorselessly attacking the President in his first major speech. The same kind of thing had been said repeatedly by other Whigs. The speech therefore brought him no kudos and, in fact, did him a great deal of harm.

In his own state he found himself almost universally unpopular. The Democrats denounced him as a disgrace. He was referred to as a modern Benedict Arnold, a synonym for a traitor. His so-called

American troops under General Winfield Scott landing at Vera Cruz during the Mexican War of 1846-8. Lincoln strongly criticized America's part in the war, declaring in the House of Representatives that 'the war with Mexico was unnecessary and unconstitutionally commenced by the President'. (Anne S. K. Brown Military Collection)

'Spot' resolutions were exploited malevolently. A paper called him the 'ranchero spotty'. A peculiar disease called spotted fever was prevalent in Michigan, and the *State Register* remarked with gusto:

This fever does not prevail to any very alarming extent in Illinois. The only case we have heard of that is likely to prove fatal is that of 'spotty Lincoln', of this State. This 'spotty' gentleman had a severe attack of 'spotted fever' in Washington City not long since and fears were entertained that the disease would 'strike in' and carry him off. We have not heard of any other person in Washington being on the 'spotted list' – and it is probable that the disease died with the patient – what an epitaph 'Died of Spotted Fever.'

Poor Lincoln; the nickname 'Spotty Lincoln' stuck, with disastrous consequences for him.

Billy Herndon warned his partner that public opinion in the constituency was outraged, but Lincoln was adamant in defending his line of conduct as the only one possible. 'Would you have voted what you felt you knew to be a lie? I know you would have not. Would you have gone out of the House and skulked the vote? I expect not. If you had skulked one vote you would have had to skulk many more. Richardson's resolutions make a direct question of the justice of the war, so that no man can be silent if he would. You are compelled to speak and your only alternative is to tell the truth or tell a lie.' There blazes out the man of conscience inside the rising young politician, and the rising young politician paid what seemed for years to have been a ruinous price.

Lincoln did not merely fade out of Congress and automatically return to full-time practice; the sequence of events was not quite so simple. A big issue during the first session of Congress was the Presidential election of 1848. Lincoln realized that his admired Henry Clay had no chance of winning. The name of General Taylor, the hero of the Mexican War, was eagerly promoted. 'Old Rough and Ready' was hardly a Whig type, a slave-owner, an advocate of annexation of Mexican territory and an exponent of the military spirit that the Whigs denounced. But he seemed at that moment to be the one man who could win the election for the Whigs. Lincoln did everything he could to rally support for him in Illinois. He swung the Illinois delegation to Taylor at the national convention. He spoke for him in Washington, Massachusetts, Chicago and elsewhere, with doubtful impact. His own opposition to the Mexican War was naturally used heavily against him. Nevertheless, Taylor was duly elected President and Lincoln took justifiable pride in the Illinois vote.

When Lincoln's term in Congress ended, he was hopeful that his labours on behalf of Taylor would obtain their reward. The appointment of the Commissioner of the General Land Office had been promised to Illinois. Lincoln backed an Illinois candidate, but when a Chicago lawyer called Butterfield intervened, he felt free to go after the job himself. On his own behalf he canvassed almost frantically it seems, circularizing politicians, soliciting signatures and rushing to Washington. Butterfield won and Lincoln lost, but the trip to Washington left behind it at least one good anecdote. The only other passenger in the stage-coach for a good proportion of the journey was a Kentuckian. He offered

54

Lincoln a chew of tobacco. With a plain 'No, Sir, I never chew', he declined, and a long silence followed. Later the Kentuckian offered Lincoln a cigar, which he also politely declined on the ground that he never smoked. Finally, as they neared the station where horses were to be changed, he poured out a cup of brandy and offered it to Lincoln with the remark: 'Well, stranger, seeing you don't smoke or chew, perhaps you'll take a little of this French brandy – it's the prime article and a good appetiser besides.' Lincoln, how-ever, declined in the same fashion as before. When they separated, the Kentuckian shook Lincoln warmly by the hand and said to him good humouredly: 'See here stranger, you're a clever but strange companion. I may never see you again, and I don't want to offend you, but I want to say this: my experience has taught me that the man who has no vices has damn few virtues. Good day!' Lincoln took great pleasure in telling this story.

There is another negative footnote to be added. Lincoln, at this point, was offered the secretaryship of Oregon which would soon become a fully-fledged state, when he himself would become Governor. Lincoln was tempted, but Mrs Lincoln vetoed the pro-position. The return to Springfield after the high hopes she had formed of life in Washington must have contained its own bitter-ness, but she had faith in her husband's political future after he himself had lost it. On this occasion at least she rendered a lasting service.

The years 1849-54 are the years of Lincoln's withdrawal from politics, or the withdrawal of politics from him. Who can say whether, deep down, he cherished a hope or plan of one day returning to public life? The evidence and the authorities point the other way.

One learned writer has described Lincoln as a man who passed through periods of ebb and flow, and sees 1849-54 as a striking example of the former. Benjamin Thomas, on the other hand, sees these years as among the most fruitful of his life: 'As he put aside all thought of political advancement and devoted himself to personal improvement, he grew tremendously in mind and character.' Certainly when he reappears in 1854 the public is conscious of an altogether bigger personality. The creative pause seems to have worked wonders. It is not clear, however, how far he set out deliberately to improve himself. Herndon insists that he was not, and never became in any sense, well read. As a boy he had astonished everyone by his addiction to the Bible, and a few classics. 'But in his maturity', says Herndon, beyond a limited acquaintance with Shakespeare, Byron and Burns, 'Mr Lincoln comparatively speaking had no knowledge of literature ... he never in his life sat down and read a book through, yet he readily could quote any number of passages from the few volumes whose pages he had hastily scanned.' Even if we confined this verdict to the years when Herndon knew him well, we must accept it as somewhere near the truth.

It was said of him, however, that he read less and thought more than any man in America. His power of thought, of argumentative reasoning, seems to have been deliberately developed in relation to the law, and more widely. Herndon gives a vivid picture of occupying the same bed with him on circuit: 'his long legs causing his feet to hang over the end'. Herndon would be sound asleep, while Lincoln would go on studying for hours. In this way he studied Euclid 'until he could with ease demonstrate all the propositions in the six books' (this was one volume at least which he did read right through). He had plenty of time to ponder deeply the eternal verities as he rode on circuit through the fourteen counties of central and eastern Illinois for at least half the year. The external sign was a marked progress in his profession.

Much argument has raged around the question of Lincoln's prowess as a lawyer. Judge David Davis, before whom he appeared on innumerable occasions, said in the eulogy of him at Indianapolis in 1865: 'In all the elements that constituted a lawyer, he had few equals. He was great at *nisi prius* and before an appellate tribunal.' 'Lincoln', he said, saw the strong points of a cause and presented them with clearness and great compactness. His mind was logical and direct. An unfailing vein of humour never deserted him.' That was said in a panegyric within a year of Lincoln's death. Judge Davis qualified it privately to Herndon. 'Mr Lincoln', he said, 'had no managing faculty, nor organizing power, hence a child could conform to the simple and technical rules, the means and the modes of getting at justice better than he. The law has its own rules, and the student could get at them or keep with them better than Lincoln.' Herndon accepts this assessment, and supplements it in his own words: 'He was at the same time a very great and a very insignificant lawyer.'

A young man once wrote to Lincoln, enquiring how best to obtain a thorough knowledge of the law. 'The mode is very simple', he replied, 'though laborious and tedious. It is only to get books and read and study them carefully through, say twice. Take

William Herndon, who for sixteen years was Lincoln's law partner. In 1889 he published one of the best-known and most controversial biographies of Lincoln. (Lincoln National Life Foundation, Fort Wayne, Ind.)

up Chitty's Pleadings, Greenleaf's Evidence and Story's Equity in succession. Work, work, work is the main thing.' Herndon will not accept this as it stands. He doubted whether Lincoln ever read a single elementary law book, 'in fact, I may truthfully say I never knew him to read through a law book of any kind'. But he adds this important proviso: 'When he had occasion to investigate or learn any subject, he was thorough and indefatigable in his search. He not only went to the roots of any question, but dug up the root and separated and analysed every fibre.' In his advice then to work, work, work, Lincoln was not exaggerating his own exertions. Perhaps, however, like other self-educated men, he tried to

57

persuade himself that he possessed a knowledge of intellectual principles which was not his. His outstanding merit lay rather in his capacity to apply to each particular case his extraordinary mind and personality. Speaking generally, Herndon noticed a marked change in his approach to the law after his disappearance from politics. 'He was not soured at his seeming political decline, but still he determined to eschew politics from that time forward, and devote himself entirely to the law. And now he began to make up for time lost in politics by studying the law in earnest', no doubt in its practical rather than theoretical bearings.

Judge Davis, in criticizing Lincoln's lack of method, was referring it would seem to his performance in court. The same could be said, and more so, of the way he ran his office. There was, in fact, no order in the office at all. The firm of Lincoln & Herndon kept no books; they divided their fees without taking any receipts or making any entries. A student who worked there for some years recalls: 'One day Mr Lincoln received $5,000 as a fee in a railroad case. He came in and said: "Well, Billy," addressing his partner, Mr Herndon, "here is our fee; sit down and let me divide." He counted out $2,500 to his partner, and gave it to him with as much nonchalance as he would have given a few cents for a paper. Cupidity had no abiding place in his nature.'

One point about his forensic effectiveness seemed generally agreed on. 'In order', said Judge Davis, 'to bring into full activity his great powers, it was necessary that he should be convinced of the right and justice of the matter which he advocated.' The other side of that coin was his inability to argue a case strongly or, indeed, proceed with it if he did not believe in it. He once wrote to a client: 'I do not think that there is the least use of doing anything more with your lawsuit. I not only do not think you are sure to gain it, but I do think you are sure to lose it, therefore the sooner it ends the better.' His retention to defend a lawsuit did not prevent him from throwing it up in its most critical stage if he believed he was espousing an unjust cause; if he felt that he had actually been deceived by a client his wrath was terrible. On one occasion of this kind, he left the court-room refusing to return. To the messenger who came to fetch him from the tavern, he said: 'Tell the judge that I can't come – my hands are dirty and I came over to clean them.'

The same fierce anger could blaze out on behalf of an exploited client. To quote Judge Davis again: 'When in a lawsuit he believed his client was oppressed, as in the Wright case, he was hurtful in denunciation. When he attacked meanness, fraud or

58

vice, he was powerful, merciless in his castigation.' In the Wright case, Lincoln set out to compel a pension agent (Wright) to refund half the pension of the widow of a revolutionary soldier which he had kept for himself. He said to Herndon: 'I am going to skin Wright and get that money back.' And skin him he did, remorselessly. But Lincoln's peroration on behalf of the widow is of still greater interest; it demonstrates that the immortal oratory of Gettysburg and the inaugurals did not spring up from nowhere:

Time rolls by [he concluded], the heroes of '76 have passed away. The soldier has gone to rest and now, crippled, blinded and broken, his widow comes to you and to me, gentlemen of the jury, to right her wrongs. She was not always thus. She was once a beautiful young woman. Her step was elastic, her face as fair and her voice as sweet as any that rang in the mountains of old Virginia. But now she is poor and defenceless. Out here on the prairies of Illinois, many hundreds of miles away from the scenes of her childhood, she appeals to us who enjoy the privileges achieved for us by the patriots of the Revolution for our sympathetic aid and manly protection. All I ask is, shall we befriend her?

The same emotional eloquence, based this time on a long-standing affection, was exhibited in a famous murder trial. William Armstrong, his client, was the harum scarum son of his old friend, originally his wrestling opponent of New Salem days, Jack Armstrong. Lincoln responded immediately, waiving any thought of a fee, to his widow's desperate appeal. With the help of an almanac, he proved that the night was far too dark for the main witness to have seen Armstrong strike the fatal blow. But what was remembered long afterwards was the peroration. He told the jury of his once being a poor, friendless boy, that Armstrong's parents took him into their house, fed and clothed him. There were tears in his eyes as he spoke; the sight of his tall, quivering frame, and the particulars of the story he so pathetically told, moved the jury to tears also, and they forgot the guilt of the defendant in their admiration of his advocate. So wrote one who ought to know. He was the prosecuting attorney who lost a case through Lincoln's *tour de force*, which he must have felt sure of winning.

The largest fee Lincoln ever earned was the $5,000 already mentioned. It was paid by the Illinois Central Railway when he won a case involving the right of McLean County to tax the railway's property. The railways were still in their pioneer stage and many of the legal decisions affecting them owed much to Lincoln's arguments and provided future precedents. He appeared for many other corporations, though never exclusively a corporation

59

ILLINOIS CENTRAL RAILROAD COMPANY
OFFER FOR SALE
ONE MILLION ACRES OF SUPERIOR FARMING LANDS,
IN FARMS OF
40, 80 & 160 acres and upwards at from $8 to $12 per acre
THESE LANDS ARE
NOT SURPASSED BY ANY IN THE WORLD.

An advertisement for the Illinois Central Railroad Company which paid Lincoln the highest fee he ever earned as a lawyer, $5,000. (Allegheny College, Tarbell Collection)

lawyer. Thomas says that he now ranked as a distinguished lawyer in a state that boasted an unusual array of outstanding legal talent. But his local repute still had limits, as the outcome of his largest patent case was to demonstrate painfully. A number of companies were involved. Eminent counsel were employed on both sides. Lincoln was originally brought in as a local lawyer in good standing with the court in Chicago, where the case was to be held. In the event, it was transferred to Cincinnati. The presence of Lincoln, who had already worked hard on the case, became strictly speaking, unnecessary. Either Lincoln or Stanton, a lawyer of much wider national reputation, had to drop out. In one way or another, Lincoln found himself discarded. He stayed around, anxious as always to benefit from experience, but left Cincinnati with feelings of rare bitterness. Lincoln felt that Stanton had been very discourteous and that he had received disagreeable treatment

60

on all sides. Stanton, it is said, described him as 'a long, lank creature from Illinois, wearing a dirty linen duster for a coat, on the back of which the perspiration had splotched wide stains that resembled a map of the Continent'. It is not clear how much of this reached Lincoln immediately, but on his return, though keeping rather quiet about the whole incident, he told Herndon that he had 'been roughly handled by that man Stanton'. He overheard Stanton saying about himself: 'Where did that long-armed creature come from and what can he expect to do in this case?' A member of the Cincinnati borough recalled that 'Mr Lincoln remained in Cincinnati about a week, moving freely around, yet not twenty men knew him personally, or knew he was here; not a hundred would have known who he was, had his name been given to them.' Yet, little more than three years later, he was elected President of the United States. Lincoln seems to have been impressed intellectually by some of the advocates, but not by the judge. He characterized him as an old granny, with no perception at all. 'If you were to point your finger at him', he said, 'and a darning needle at the same time, he never would know which was the sharpest.'

3 The Call to the Summit 1854-60

LINCOLN HAD RETIRED FROM POLITICS but politics declined to follow his example. By 1850 tension was rising fast between North and South. The drive to the West went on remorselessly, producing new interests and problems at every turn. By now all sorts of economic issues were involved but slavery was the urgent point of conflict. In this year a second compromise, complementing, or as some would say supplanting, the Missouri Compromise of 1820, was reached, at the instigation of the great Whig compromiser Henry Clay. California was to be admitted as a free state and the slave trade was to be stopped in the district of Columbia. These steps would please the North. On the other hand, to placate the South, the rest of the land taken from Mexico was to be organized into territories with no provision as to slavery or its absence. A most strict law was to be passed, enforcing the return of fugitive slaves. In the election campaign of 1852, in which Lincoln took a rather languid part, both parties appeared to be pleased with the compromise. When Clay died in the same year, Lincoln paid him a heartfelt tribute.

And then, almost out of the blue, although the operation took a little time to complete, Senator Douglas secured the passage of a Bill which empowered the people of Kansas to decide for themselves whether they would permit slavery or not. Under the existing compromise, slavery would be ruled out in their area. The cataclysmic effect of this measure cannot be exaggerated. It expressly repealed the hard-won understanding on which for thirty-five years the whole balance of the American fabric had depended.

Senator Douglas was, by any reckoning, an outstanding American of this period. No more than five feet tall, but enormously strong with a tremendous voice, he was known as 'the Little Giant' and was at all times forceful and fearless. His career ran on parallel lines with that of Lincoln. In the 1830s they had both been members of the Illinois State Assembly. In 1838 they were admitted to practise in the Supreme Court of Illinois on the same day. In 1842 Lincoln had won the hand of Mary Todd after Douglas had, to say the least, been warmly interested. In 1846 Douglas represented Illinois in the United States Senate, Lincoln in the House of Representatives. In 1858 Lincoln stood against Douglas unsuccessfully for the Senate; in 1860 successfully for the Presidency. In 1854, when the contest between the two men began, the advantage had lain strongly with Douglas, a US Senator for the last eight years as compared with Lincoln, a busy provincial lawyer who had

PREVIOUS PAGES Republican rally outside Lincoln's home in Springfield, Illinois in August 1860. Lincoln can be seen in a white coat standing to the right of his front door. (Courtesy Chicago Historical Society)

had his chance in politics and disappeared from the national scene.

Douglas's motives for introducing his very controversial Bill have been endlessly discussed. It is easy to derive them from the current controversy about the route to be taken by the projected trans-continental railway. Should it pursue a southern course from New Orleans or run from Chicago through Nebraska and Salt Lake City to San Francisco? Various leading Democrats preferred the former but Douglas favoured the latter route. On this theory Douglas's so-called Kansas–Nebraska Bill must be seen as part of his attempt to secure Southern support for his purpose. That formulation, while not inaccurate, appears to understate his idealism. One has no reason to doubt his statement in the Senate that it was a bill 'very dear to his heart; of immense magnitude and great import to the entire nation'. Nothing meant so much to him, apart from the preservation of the Union, as his Western

Henry Clay in Congress defending his resolutions which were to become the basis of the five statutes, known as the Compromise of 1850, designed to resolve the slavery issue. Lincoln, a great admirer of Clay, later said of this measure: 'The nation has passed its perils, and is free, prosperous and powerful.' (Radio Times Hulton Picture Library)

programme, his dream of strengthening the United States through
the development, in Professor Johannsen's phrase, 'of its great
Western potential'. Unless the South could be won over, 'there
was no possibility that organized Government could be brought
to the central plains'. He was far too shrewd, however, to be
unaware that his Bill would create a storm. His expectations were
fulfilled more than amply.

The impact on Lincoln was traumatic. The news of its passage
through Congress roused him, he said, 'as he had never been
before'. Three months later, he was back in politics. In the office
discussions, Herndon recalls 'that he grew bolder in his utterances'.
He insisted that the social and political differences between slavery
and freedom were becoming more marked; that one must overcome
the other; and that postponing the struggle between them would
only make it the more deadly in the end. 'The day of compromise',

he contended, 'has passed. These two great ideas have been kept apart only by the most artful means. They are like two wild beasts in sight of each other, but chained and held apart. Some day these deadly antagonists will one or the other break their bonds, and then the question will be settled.'

From now increasingly till 1860 we find Lincoln almost incessantly occupied at conventions, at public meetings, in correspondence and in secret consultation.

The old Whig Party had been falling apart since 1852. Their great chieftains Clay and Webster were dead. The authors of the 1850 Compromise saw it as essential to the preservation of the Union but it led directly to the destruction of the Whig Party. The gap between North and South was becoming too great. 'Finality', so ardently claimed for the 1850 Compromise, was seen to be a chimera. Now the Southern members were deserting to the Democratic Party, and the Northern ones to all sorts of anti groups: anti-immigrants, anti-drink, abolitionists and anti-slavery-in-the-new-territories. There was a fine opportunity for a unifying cause and, in fact, a whole variety of elements came together in vehement hostility to Douglas's sabotage of the Missouri Compromise. In February 1854, while the Kansas–Nebraska Bill was still before the Senate, a heterogeneous but significant group resolved, if the measure went through, to throw old Party organizations to the winds, and organize a new party on the sole basis of the non-extension of slavery. The first national convention of this new Republican Party met in Pittsburg in 1856. By 1860, it had developed a well-rounded economic programme, calculated to appeal to the Northern states, but its essential message was twofold: the Union must not be dissolved; and slavery must not spread into new territories.

Lincoln was not one of the founder members of the new Republican Party, but in 1856 in Illinois and beyond he became one of its leading activists. In 1854, still a Whig, he challenged Douglas to a prolonged mortal combat that continued up to and into the Presidential contest of 1860. He knew Douglas of old, liked him very well on the whole but rated him poorly as a man of political principle. He had never felt himself in any way his inferior and seized with both hands the chance to do battle with his famous opponent in front of a national audience.

The question of Lincoln's own ambition must be touched on. 'The man', says Herndon, 'who thinks Lincoln calmly sat down

him has a very erroneous knowledge of Lincoln. He was always calculating and always planning ahead. His ambition was a little engine that knew no rest. But that is only a part, and perhaps a minor part, of the truth.' It has been said before now that real statesmen are dominated by two motives only: 'love of country and love of power'. There is no doubt that, as time went on, he was ready to assume any responsibilities for which his friends thought him qualified, and manifestly eager to do so. Herndon, however, demonstrates convincingly that Lincoln's tremendous and far-reaching reaction to Douglas's Bill was based on a moral conviction concerning the injustice of human slavery.

With the adjournment of Congress, Douglas returned to Illinois to defend his record, by now violently opposed by what he called 'the allied forces of abolitionism, Whigism, nativism and religious intolerance'. At the same time many of the Southern Democrats felt that he had given away far too much and weakened the cause for slavery. On 3 October 1854 Douglas addressed a huge meeting in Springfield. Lincoln waited outside and announced that he would reply next day. Again the hall was packed as Lincoln, in shirt-sleeves and without collar and tie, delivered an impressive harangue, with Douglas sitting in the front row. His speech was not reported in its entirety until repeated twelve days later at Peoria. It has gone down to history as his Peoria Address. We are told that he began haltingly and his voice was shrill, but as he proceeded his hesitancy disappeared and his tones became better modulated. Soon he was wet with sweat and his matted hair became tousled as he flung back his head.

Striking events were to occur between October 1854 and his election campaign for the Presidency six years later. His general standpoint, however, can be said to have been unfolded once and for all in the address at Peoria. Now, for the first time (but he was to repeat the point interminably), he distinguished clearly between his attitude towards the extension of slavery and his position with respect to slavery where it already existed. 'If all earthly powers were given me, I would not know what to do as to the existing situation.' His first impulse was to free the slaves and send them to Liberia, where the American Colonization Society had established a Negro republic. But he granted that whatever hope this might offer as a long-range solution, its immediate accomplishment was physically impossible. 'I think I would not hold one in slavery, at any rate,' he said, as though he were thinking out the problem before his audience, 'yet that point is not clear enough for me to denounce people upon. . . . It does seem to me that some system of gradual emancipation might be adopted; but for their tardiness in this, I will not undertake to judge our brethren of the south.' Again and again, however, he came back to the intrinsic evil of slavery and passionately asserted that proposition in face of Douglas's appeal to the sacred right of self-government. The right, in other words, of a state to decide whether it would, or would not, allow slavery within its borders.

He insisted that the doctrine of self-government in its application depended

... on whether a Negro was, or was not, a man. If he is not a man, why in that case he who is a man may, as a matter of self-government, do just as he pleases with him. But if the Negro is a man, is it not to that extent a total destruction of self-government to say that he too shall not govern himself? When the white man governs himself, that is self-government; but when he governs another man, that is more than self-government – that is despotism. If the Negro is a man, why then my ancient faith teaches me that 'all men are created equal', and that there can be no moral right in connection with one man's making a slave of another.

As we read these and many other passages today, we can feel that no one ever put the anti-slavery case more powerfully, and yet in the 1850s he was still sharply opposing the abolitionists, his young friend Herndon among them. Certain rights, he kept on repeating, including the right to operate slavery if they chose, had been guaranteed to the states of the Union. It would be a breach of the Constitution and a breach of the moral law to over-ride those rights. Emancipation, he hoped and believed, would come about in the process of time, but in a far better way for the slaves as well as for their masters if it were voluntary. Some words of his (used on a later occasion), read oddly today: 'I do not mean that when it takes a turn towards ultimate extinction it will be in a day, nor in a year, nor in two years. I do not suppose that in the most peaceful way ultimate extinction would occur in less than a hundred years at least; but that it will occur in the best way for both races in God's own good time I have no doubt.' Taking his speech at Peoria as a whole, we can fairly accept it as a speech of reconciliation and in that sense the new note for which men had been waiting.

Bearing in mind the key passages already quoted, there is no need to dwell in length on the argumentation of the next few years. Lincoln was now a recognized force. He was elected to the state legislature, but turned down the seat in the hopes of entering the Senate. In 1855 he found himself out-manœuvred. He showed considerable altruism or foresight in persuading his supporters to vote for an anti-Douglas Democrat. For five more years, however, he was compelled to earn his living at the law, from 1856 a committed Republican.

Meanwhile, apart from all sorts of other ructions, an extra-ordinary judgment had been given in March 1857 by Chief Justice Taney in the famous Dred Scott case which was concerned with a fugitive slave. The various dicta in the case were as provocative as the decision itself. At the time of the adoption of the Constitution, said the Chief Justice, Negroes were looked on as such inferior beings that they had no rights which the white man was bound to respect. They were not included within the meaning of the pronouncement of Independence that 'all men are created equal'. This was, of course, in flat contradiction to Lincoln's belief already quoted. Scott, not being a citizen, had no right to sue in a federal court. The case must be dismissed. The judge did not end there. He went on to declare that the Missouri Compromise was void. Slaves were property and Congress had no power to exclude them from a territory. The same was true of a territorial legislature. If this decision were to prevail, the whole of the United States would henceforth be open to slavery without restriction. The Republicans were naturally furious.

We learn without surprise that Lincoln came forward in the year 1858 to oppose Douglas for the Senate. The step required considerable initiative. The leading Republicans in the Eastern states were inclined to welcome Douglas to the Republican ranks, as someone basically anti-slavery and already on bad terms with the Southern Democrats. But the Republican leaders in Illinois remained staunchly loyal to Lincoln. There followed seven historic debates between Lincoln and Douglas. Both the champions stuck closely to the question of slavery. Lincoln and Douglas both believed in free homesteads and in internal improvements at Federal expense. Both were strongly pro-Union, so slavery provided the two orators with a genuine area of argument.

Douglas was embarrassed by the Dred Scott decision of Taney. Nor was he unaware of his adversary's quality. When he heard of Lincoln's nomination, he predicted, 'I shall have my hands full. He is the strong man of his Party, full of wit, facts, dates and the best stump-speaker in the West, with his droll ways and dry jokes.' Vast crowds assembled to listen. Ten thousand at Ottawa, fifteen thousand at Freeport, twelve to fifteen thousand at Charleston. Bands, military companies and cavalcades of horsemen headed long processions escorting the speakers. Fireworks, rockets and cannon flared and boomed. At one place Lincoln rode in a wagon drawn by six white horses. With ever-developing literary skill and tireless dialectic, he spelled out the same case, so passionate and yet so balanced, that he had propounded four years earlier at Peoria.

The most famous phrase he used was one which stirred deep feelings, but was capable of misunderstanding:

The house divided against itself [he quoted from the Gospel] cannot stand. I believe this Government cannot endure permanently half slave and half free. I do not expect the Union to be dissolved. I do not expect the house to fall, but I do expect it will cease to be divided. It will become all one thing or all the other. Either the opponents of slavery will arrest the further spread of it and place it where the public mind shall rest, in the belief that it is in course of ultimate extinction; or its advocates will push it forward, till it shall become alike lawful in all the States, old as well as new, North as well as South.

Douglas took him up on the phrase 'a house divided against itself', as he was entitled to. Why could the nation not continue part slave and part free, as it had for eighty-two years? Uniformity of local institutions was neither essential nor desirable. Lincoln claimed that he had been misunderstood. He had merely offered a prediction, 'it may have been a foolish one'. He had not expressed a wish. He had said a hundred times that the people of the North should not meddle with slavery in the states where it existed, but if slavery were confined within its existing limits it would be 'put in course of ultimate extinction'. One cannot help feeling that someone who detested slavery as much as Lincoln was on very thin ice here. This side of Lincoln's doctrine is apt to jar upon us today, but at the time the bold statement that a house divided against itself could not stand gave great comfort to the side of freedom.

Lincoln came quite close to winning. The Republican legislative candidates polled more votes than their opponents, but the electoral law favoured the Democratic districts. The vote in the legislature was fifty-four for Douglas and forty-six for Lincoln. The latter, however, had won national *réclame*. Later on, he recalls that he said to himself, 'It's a slip and not a fall.' At the time he wrote to a friend: 'I am glad that I made the late race. It gave me a hearing on the great and durable question of the age which I could have had in no other way, and though I now sink out of view and shall be forgotten, I believe that I have made some marks which

71

Lincoln and Douglas debating in Illinois in 1858. The famous series of debates between the two men established Lincoln as a great speaker and well-known personality in Illinois, if not nationally. (American Museum of Photography)

will tell for the cause of civil liberty long after I am gone.' So speak and write even the best of politicians. Within two years, in November 1860, he was elected President.

For the next few months, events rolled forward towards a collision between North and South. John Brown, a puritanical anti-slavery fanatic, gathered a small party of deluded followers, invaded the slave area, seized Harpers Ferry and seemed to the South to be embarked on a slave uprising. Earlier he and his sons had killed five unarmed men in cold blood. He was easily overcome by the Federal forces, but he held out to the last, desperately wounded, one son dead and one dying beside him. He was finally hanged, rejoicing as he went to his death: 'You may dispose of me', he said, 'very easily. I am nearly disposed of now, but this Negro question is still to be settled. The end of that is not yet.'

Lincoln, in his speeches that autumn (1859), paid tribute to Brown's rare courage and unselfishness, but described his lawlessness as indefensible. 'The North', he said, 'could raise no objection to Brown's execution.' Opposition to slavery could never justify violence, bloodshed and treason. But the same moral must be understood by the South. If they should set out to destroy the Union, it would be just as unconstitutional. 'It would be our duty to deal with you as old John Brown has been dealt with.' At this stage Lincoln might be said to stand, before all else, for law and order, that is for enforcing the Constitution. But the passions were mounting on each side which would rule out a specific settlement.

At what point did he begin to entertain serious hopes of becoming President? More than once during 1859 we find him resisting the suggestion from local admirers. An editor, Thomas Pickett, proposed to come out publicly on his behalf; Lincoln begged him not to: 'I must in candour say I am not fit for the Presidency.' And with regard to a concerted effort for the same purpose: 'I really think it best for our cause that no concerted effort such as you suggest should be made.' But he lost no opportunity of speaking in Illinois and other states. Herndon recalls him 'rushing into the office with an invitation to deliver a major address in New York'. A date was fixed for February 1860. Lincoln devoted himself to careful preparation. He rightly surmised that his future hung on the outcome. The speech was delivered at the Cooper Union on 27 February 1860, before what the renowned editor Horace Greeley called 'the largest assemblage of the intellect and culture of our city since the days of Clay and Webster'. It was an unqualified personal success.

Lincoln speaking at the
Cooper Union on the evening
of 27 February 1860. This
speech made him famous in
the East. The New York
Tribune reported: 'He's the
greatest man since St Paul.
No man ever before made
such an impression on his
first appeal to a New York
audience.' (Cooper Union)

In a sense Lincoln was only developing a theme that he had
already promulgated quite often. The double message, however,
was never perhaps spelled out so powerfully till the end of the Civil
War. He spoke of the Southern people as a reasonable and just
people and begged his own friends to treat them as such: 'Even
though much provoked, let us do nothing through passion and ill-
temper. . . . We must not only let them [the South] alone, but we
must somehow convince them that we do let them alone. . . . Wrong
as we think slavery is, we can yet afford to let it alone where it is,
because that much is due to the necessity arising from its actual
presence in the nation.' But never in any circumstances must they
disguise their deeply held conviction that the institution of slavery
was intrinsically evil:

76

Their thinking it right, and our thinking it wrong, is the precise fact upon which depends the whole controversy. Thinking it right, as they do, they are not to blame for desiring its full recognition as being right; but thinking it wrong, as we do, can we yield to them? Can we cast our votes with their view and against our own? In view of our moral, social and political responsibilities, can we do this? ... Let us have faith that right makes might and in that faith let us to the end dare to do our duty as we understand it.

Lincoln had been initially nervous, unusually so. He had feared that his Western accent and mannerisms might seem laughable to the sophisticated East. His new broadcloth suit seemed to fit him as badly as his previous garments. But as he proceeded, these trivialities were soon forgotten by himself and his audience. When he came to the end with the peroration quoted, men and women rose to their feet shouting, waving hats and handkerchiefs in the stormy applause which quickly became an ovation. The New York papers printed the speech in full with enthusiastic comments. Seldom, we are told, has a visitor made such a profound impression on a New York audience; as Herndon says: 'He had captured the metropolis.' He followed it with other telling addresses, before going back to Springfield in triumph.

When Lincoln returned to Springfield, he made no further attempt to disguise his opinion that a Presidential nomination was within his grasp. 'He wrote', says Herndon, 'to encourage Party workers everywhere.' Early in the year a group of Lincoln's friends had come together to promote his candidature. The Illinois State Convention of the Republican Party was their first objective. In the event, the meeting was made memorable by Lincoln's cousin, John Hanks. He electrified the audience by producing two rails which he and Lincoln, said he, had made together in Sangamon. Deafening applause. 'These rails', said a delegate, 'were to represent the issue in the coming contest between labour free and labour slave, between democracy and aristocracy.' His next comment shows how even his admirers still found it difficult to see Lincoln as a President. 'Little did I think', he went on, 'that the tall and angular and bony rail splitter who stood in girlish diffidence, bowing with awkward grace, would fill the chair once filled by Washington.' Lincoln was induced to say a few words of thanks; he could not say whether he had made those rails, 'but he had surely mauled better ones.' Loud and renewed applause. The nickname of Rail Splitter stuck to him, the ideal image, as we would now say, for the champion of the common man.

Photograph of Lincoln taken in 1860. (Lincoln National Life Foundation, Fort Wayne, Ind.)

Lincoln's most formidable adversary as Presidential candidate appeared to be William H. Seward, an ex-Governor of New York, and for quite some years a Senator. He was friendly and sociable, but in Agar's phrase 'tormentingly ambitious'. A man of high ability, he had been aiming for a long time at the White House. He had been the Whig Party leader in the Senate after the deaths of Clay and Webster and saw himself as the natural leader of the Republicans. He had made a national reputation by his attack on slavery. He had spoken far more sympathetically of John Brown than had Lincoln, and was famous among many other things for his notable phrase 'the irrepressible conflict'. Another powerful and distinguished abolitionist who, like Seward, had opposed the Compromise of 1850 as too favourable to slavery, was Salmon P. Chase. He was deeply religious in a sanctimonious way, but convinced of his duty to become President. He had joined in his time party after party: the Whigs, the anti-immigrant party calling itself American and, finally, the all-embracing Republicans. He sounds extraordinarily unattractive, but was a brilliant man and in his own way high principled. Seward, however, was from Lincoln's point of view the main danger.

In spite of his shining success in New York, Lincoln, compared with his opponents, was still relatively unknown in the country when the Republican Convention met in May at Chicago. Nor would he have an opportunity of making a personal appeal to the delegates. If he was to win, it must be as a man who was likely to secure more votes than any other candidate. If Douglas had been the sole Democratic candidate, the Republicans would not have had much of an outlook. But Douglas was, by this time, deep in trouble with his own party, especially the Southern leaders. They wanted something much more favourable to slavery than his doctrine of popular sovereignty, i.e. leaving it to the states to decide. They claimed, with some legal reason, that the Dred Scott decision made it impossible for a state to abolish slavery, even if it wished to. The Democratic vote was certain to be split. The Republicans were 'in with a chance', if they acted wisely.

Lincoln, as always, assessed his prospects coolly. 'My name', he wrote, 'is new in the field and I suppose that I am not the first choice of a great many. Our policy then is to give no offence to others. Leave them in a mood to come in if they shall be impelled to give up their first love.' And this strategy in fact prevailed all the more because it so clearly expressed not only his self-interest but his convictions. No one could doubt by this time his detestation

of slavery, but his conciliatory attitude towards the South, his
refusal to set about destroying slavery where it already existed,
was reckoned rightly to be a winning card in the crucial border-
line areas. The Convention, however, was certainly no walk-over.

On 16 May, ten thousand people filled the vast pineboard
structure known as the Wigwam, with twice as many outside.
Excitement mounted unbearably in the hall, while every kind of
manœuvre was embarked on behind the scenes. On the first
count Seward was $173\frac{1}{2}$, Lincoln 102, Cameron of Pennsylvania
$50\frac{1}{2}$, Chase 49, Bates 48. On the face of it, Lincoln was a long way
behind. Lincoln had sent a telegram to his supporters: 'I authorize
no bargains and will be bound by none.' But his friends, whether
or not they took the message seriously, knew better. Cameron of
Pennsylvania was promised a Cabinet post if Pennsylvania
declared for Lincoln, which was duly done. One of Lincoln's team
leaned over to whisper to the chairman of the Ohioans: 'If you can
throw the Ohio delegation to Lincoln, Chase can have anything he
wants.' The Ohio chairman, a stammerer, bounded up, exclaiming
excitedly: 'I a-a-rise, Mr Chairman, to a-a-nnounce the c-ch-change
of f-four votes from Mr Chase to Mr Lincoln.' Lincoln was through
and pandemonium took over.

Lincoln had been awaiting the result at Springfield, labouring
not surprisingly under suppressed excitement. He had been
'tossing ball', a pastime frequently indulged in by the lawyers of
that day, and had played a few games of billiards to assist his self-
control. The news of his nomination reached him while he was
seated in a large armchair in the office of the *Springfield Journal*.
He hastened away 'to tell a little woman down the street the news'.

Next day a committee from the Convention called on him at his
home. As he listened to a short congratulatory speech, he looked
embarrassed and irresolute, but when it finished, his body
straightened to its full height. 'The dull eyes lighted with intelligence that animated the whole countenance. The irresolute figure
took on a calm, sure dignity.' His words in reply made a lasting
impression. One of the committee men said to another, as he walked
down the street: 'Well, we might have done a more brilliant thing,
but we certainly could not have done a better thing.' He had
insisted on their joining him in refreshments – a glass of water all
round.

Now the battle for the Presidency began in earnest. In those
days, there was a tradition that a candidate refrained from cam-
paigning on his own behalf. Lincoln therefore remained quietly in

The Election of 1860

When someone suggested to Lincoln in 1859 that he might be the Republican nominee for President, he replied 'I do not think myself fit for the Presidency.' Soon, however, his opinion changed and he was supporting his friends in their efforts to bring his name forward. At the Republican Convention in Chicago in May 1860 Lincoln secured the

nomination, after several ballots and the usual conferences and bargainings. The Democratic Party – torn apart by the issue of slavery – had three Presidential candidates and so Lincoln's successful election in November was almost a foregone conclusion.

THE NATIONAL GAME. THREE "OUTS" AND ONE "RUN".
ABRAHAM WINNING THE BALL.

ABOVE Currier and Ives cartoon on the 1860 Presidential campaign. The winner, Lincoln, is shown on the right, with the three losers (from left to right) Bell, Douglas and Breckinridge. (Doyle De Witt Collection)

RIGHT Campaign flag for the 1860 Presidential election. Lincoln's christian name was misspelt – he did not become a nationally known figure until well on in the campaign. (Doyle De Witt Collection)

TOP RIGHT Ferrotypes of Lincoln and Douglas made for the 1860 Presidential campaign. The pictures were photographed in tin and set in brass frames. They were intended to be worn as lapel ornaments. (Doyle De Witt Collection)

Springfield. He issued no statement of policy. He pointed out that he had already fully defined his position. He seems to have been happy with the Republican programme, carefully framed to appeal to the main sections. Agar describes their programme as one of the most coherent in American history: defence of the Union; prohibition of slavery in the territories; condemnation of the Dred Scott decision; a Pacific railway and other internal improvements; a Homestead Act and a higher tariff. It was slightly less emphatic in its hostility to slavery than the programme of 1856.

Meanwhile, the real calamities were occurring on the Democratic side. Douglas was vehemently opposed by the Southern extremists, who nominated John Breckinridge of Kentucky, with a platform demanding a positive protection of slavery in the territories. Another party was formed – the Constitutional Union Party, a moderate group of Whig relics who put forward Bell as candidate. Throughout the campaign, many Southern speakers insisted that a Republican victory meant secession. Lincoln seems to have thought that this could be avoided, but on such a matter at such a time, one would not expect him to show his hand.

The result was perfectly definite within the framework of the American system. Lincoln finished with 1,886,452 votes, Douglas 1,376,957, Breckinridge 849,781 and Bell 588,879. Lincoln's opponents out-polled him by almost a million, but in the electoral vote based on the states taken as a whole Lincoln won easily with 173 votes against seventy-two for Breckinridge, thirty-nine for Bell and twelve for Douglas. He hardly won a single vote in the South, but he won all the Northern states except New Jersey. Even if all his opponents had united their votes, he would still have won enough states to give him victory. The calculations of those who chose him as their standard-bearer had been fully justified.

4 The War of Brothers 1861

So THE YOUTH WHO HAD DRIFTED into New Salem without credentials from the back of nowhere was about to become one of the most powerful men in the world. But four months of impotence lay ahead of him while he awaited his inauguration. Till then, Buchanan was still the Democratic President and, on any reckoning, utterly futile. He would neither accept the idea of secession nor take any steps to check it. Inevitably, it drew nearer and nearer. For the moment, Lincoln could do nothing. He was, however, busy enough in Springfield, besieged by office seekers on behalf of themselves and other candidates. The hotels of Springfield, we are told, were filled with gentlemen 'who came with light baggage and heavy schemes'. The party had never been fed, and it was voraciously hungry. Lincoln saw and, in a sense, enjoyed the humour of it all, which may have helped him to survive the experience.

His choice of Cabinet Ministers was carefully worked out and sufficiently remarkable. Herndon, never very fair to Mrs Lincoln, records her later as saying: 'My husband places great reliance on my knowledge of human nature, often telling me, when about to make some important appointment, that he has no knowledge of men and their motives.' Herndon himself found Lincoln remarkably self-reliant in such matters. His Cabinet has been called 'a ministry of all the talents'. It was also, adds Agar, a ministry of all the self-assertive. Seward, his strongest opponent in the election, was appointed Secretary of State. He accepted after some hesitation, persuading himself that he could dominate Lincoln and be the ruler of the Cabinet. He was soon to find out his complete mistake and generously acknowledged, 'The President is the best of us.'

Lincoln was more or less committed to the appointment of Chase, another powerful abolitionist, who, like Seward, thought himself altogether superior to Lincoln, which sentiment did not, however, unite him and Seward in brotherly love. The remaining posts were allocated to cover as wide a spectrum as possible of sectional interests and opinions. Two appointments could only be justified, if at all, by promises of doubtful necessity made at the Convention. Caleb Smith, Minister of the Interior, was merely inadequate, but Cameron, Secretary for War, was a deplorable figure. 'I don't think he would steal a red hot stove', said a fellow politician from Pennsylvania, when asked about his honesty. An apology was demanded. 'Oh! well,' came the answer, 'I apologize. I said Cameron would not steal a red hot stove. I withdraw that statement.' Cameron ran true to form in the Cabinet. Corruption

PREVIOUS PAGES President Lincoln and General Scott, General-in-Chief of the US Army, reviewing troops on Pennsylvania Avenue, Washington, in 1861. Drawing by Alfred R. Waud. (Library of Congress)

88

Lincoln with his first Cabinet and General Scott. From left to right: Bates, Welles, Blair, Seward, Chase, Lincoln, Scott, Smith and Cameron. (Library of Congress)

was at once discovered in his department on a large scale. In January 1862, Lincoln packed him off as Minister to Russia, replacing him with another ex-Democrat of Ohio, Edwin Stanton.

Stanton in his own way was just as arrogant and unpleasant to deal with as Chase. It was only three years earlier that Lincoln had been humiliated by him at Cincinnati. He continued to talk about Lincoln contemptuously behind his back. But Lincoln was angelic

Crowds in Baltimore waiting for Lincoln to pass through on his way to Washington for his first inaugural. Rumours of a plot to assassinate Lincoln caused him to avoid visiting the town at the last minute – an action for which he was much criticized in the Press. (Mansell Collection)

towards him, recognizing his immense organizing ability. 'Did Stanton tell you I was a damn fool?' enquired Lincoln of an astonished tale-bearer. 'Then I expect I must be one, for he is almost always right and generally says what he means.' Dennis Hanks, Lincoln's cousin, did not form a favourable impression of Stanton whom he described as 'a frisky little Yankee with a short coat tail'. 'I asked Abe', he said once, 'why he didn't kick him out. I told him he was too fresh altogether.' Lincoln's answer was: 'If I did, Dennis, it would be difficult to find another man to fill his place.' In fact, Lincoln and Stanton struck up a highly effective relationship; Stanton played a major part in the organizing of victory. The names of the Cabinet, when one runs through them now, leave a rather bitter taste. They bear out the opinion, however, that Lincoln was uninfluenced by personal feelings in such matters and was rather less likely to appoint a friend than an enemy.

Meanwhile events were not waiting for the constitutional procedures to complete themselves. To all enquirers Lincoln gave simple advice: 'Stand firm . . . the tug has to come. Better now than any time hereafter. Hold firm as with a chain of steel.' It is frequently asserted that he neither wanted nor expected war. Of course it was the last thing he wanted, but the chance of its coming, however optimistically he spoke in public, must have

90

loomed larger and larger. In the Southern states there was a strong minority in favour of maintaining the Union, but many secessionists had long felt that it was a burden – in Agar's phrase 'an economic threat as well as an oral reproach'. Their chance had come and they did not intend to miss it. On 20 December, South Carolina seceded from the Union. Between 9 January and 1 February 1861, six other Southern states followed her example. They may have feared economic oppression, though the existing low tariff suited them. But their explicit arguments for secession were arguments in defence of slavery. They roundly condemned the North for its hostility towards the institution.

The secessionist Governors, without any attempt at negotiation, seized almost all the forts and arsenals in their areas. On 18 February, a provisional government under Jefferson Davis was established. The Confederate States of America came into existence, in total repudiation of the Union.

Lincoln was to deliver his first inaugural oration on 4 March. The day before he was to speak, a distinguished engineer officer had been sent by the Confederate authorities to make plans on the spot for an attack on Fort Sumter, the only Federal fort still holding out on Confederate territory. Meanwhile, the moment had come, none too soon, for Lincoln to leave Springfield and set out for Washington. He slipped away to Farmington, in Coles County, where he met his aged stepmother and the surviving members of the Hanks and Johnston families. He visited the grave of his father, Thomas Lincoln, which had been unmarked and neglected for almost a decade, and left directions that a suitable stone should be placed there to mark the spot. One would like to trace here some signs of regret for his earlier attitude. His stepmother gave him, we are assured, a true maternal benediction, her tears running down her cheeks.

His leave-taking of Herndon is agreeable to look back on. Before leaving, he requested that the signboard which swung on its rusty hinges at the foot of the stairway should remain. 'Let it hang there undisturbed', he said. 'Give our clients to understand that the election of a President makes no change in the firm of Lincoln and Herndon. If I live, I am coming back some time and then we'll go right on practising law as if nothing had ever happened.' Herndon had never seen him in a more cheerful mood and yet, a moment later, he was speaking of the unpleasant features surrounding the Presidential office. 'I am sick of office-holding already and I shudder when I think of the tasks that are still ahead.'

91

He had a strong feeling that he would never return alive. Herndon suggested that this sort of gloomy notion was not in keeping with the popular ideal of a President. 'But it is in keeping with my philosophy', retorted Lincoln, a somewhat cryptic saying.

Lincoln and Mrs Lincoln had already given a leaving party for about seven hundred of their friends. Mrs Lincoln was becomingly dressed, we are told, 'in a gown of white moiré silk with a full train and a small lace collar'. When he and his party reached the single passenger car which was to carry them to Washington, with melancholy gaze he faced the crowd who had come to say goodbye. 'My friends,' said he, 'no one not in my situation can appreciate my feeling of sadness at this parting. To this place and the kindness of these people I owe everything. Here I have lived a quarter of a century and have passed from a young to an old man. Here my children have been born and one is buried. I now leave, not knowing when, or whether ever, I may return, with a task before me greater than that which rested upon Washington.' He went on to affirm his confidence in the 'Divine Being', and his desire for their constant prayers. 'I bid you', he ended, 'an affectionate farewell.'

One cannot dwell on the many speeches, not by any means his best, which he delivered, and the excited receptions which he attended on his way to the capital. Warned of a threat to his life, he was persuaded to avoid Baltimore and to enter Washington unobtrusively. A rumour was widely circulated that he had come disguised in a Scottish plaid cap and un-military coat – totally untrue, of course, but he was never proud of the episode. His courage was always immaculate and it was disagreeable that his enemies should get the chance to question it.

His appearance at his first inaugural has been described by one eye-witness in particular. It should be mentioned that a little girl called Grace Bedell had written to him shortly before his election as President. 'I have four brothers and part of them will vote for you anyway, and if you will let your whiskers grow, I will try and get the rest of them to vote for you. You would look a great deal better, for your face is so thin.' Lincoln had replied : 'My dear little miss . . . as to the whiskers, having never worn any, do you not think that people would call it a piece of silly affection [sic] if I were to begin it now? Your very sincere well-wisher, A. Lincoln.' Soon after his election, he began to let his beard grow, becoming the first bearded President of the United States. The eye-witness at the inaugural considered that this change had spoiled a face

Lincoln taking the oath of
office as President of the
United States at his first
inaugural on 4 March 1861.
(Bettmann Archive)

On 20 December 1860 South Carolina seceded from the Union. Between 9 January and 1 February six other Southern states followed her. On 18 February delegates at Montgomery, Alabama, formed the Confederate States of America with Jefferson Davis as President. Four other states joined the Confederacy in the following weeks.

LEFT Banner of the South Carolina secession convention held in December 1860. Some of the slave states, which South Carolina hoped would join the new Confederacy, remained loyal to the Union. (Yale University Library)
BELOW The Confederacy started issuing its own money in 1861. (Stanley Gibbons)
RIGHT Jefferson Davis, President of the Confederate States of America. A former Senator and veteran of the Mexican War, he would have preferred a military appointment to the Presidency. (Radio Times Hulton Picture Library)

RIGHT Confederate troops firing on Fort Sumter – the incident which signalled the outbreak of the Civil War Lincoln could justifiably claim that '. . . no choice was left but to call out the war power of the Government; and so to resist force, employed for its destruction, by force, for its preservation.' (Photo Research International)
BELOW The first battle, Bull Run, fought on 21 July 1861. (Library of Congress)

which, though never handsome, had in its original state a peculiar power and pathos: 'On the present occasion the whiskers were reinforced by brand new clothing from top to toe: black dress-coat instead of the usual frock, black cloth or satin vest, black pantaloons and a glossy hat just out of the box. To cap the climax of novelty he carried a huge ebony cane with a gold head the size of an egg. In these, to him, strange habiliments, he looked so miserably uncomfortable that I could not help pitying him.' Reaching the platform, he stood there, holding his cane and hat, getting rid of the first eventually, but not knowing what to do with the second. This part of the story has a touching conclusion. Douglas, who had outdistanced him in the past and now been crushed by him, saw the President's predicament, relieved him of his hat and handed it back at the finish.

There is much noble language in the inaugural, but at the time all men read it and studied it feverishly for its immediate significance. Men of goodwill hoped against hope that war could be avoided, but everyone felt that it was perilously close, with Fort Sumter about to be attacked at any moment, unless it tamely surrendered. Was Lincoln going or not going to make it clear that Federal law and order would be enforced? If he did so at all crudely, he might lose the eight slave states which were still wavering. If he failed to do so, he would be implicitly recognizing secession and saying goodbye to the Union.

The passages which stated his immediate policy had been worked out most carefully, so as to be at once as firm and un-provocative as possible. He asserted that no state upon its own mere notion could lawfully get out of the Union. But what of those states which already considered themselves withdrawn? After all, in the preceding month they had set up their own government and formed their own confederacy. 'I shall take care', he said, 'as the Constitution itself expressly enjoins upon me, that the laws of the Union be faithfully executed in all the states. Doing this I deem to be only a simple duty on my part; and I shall perform it, so far as practicable, unless my rightful masters, the American people, shall withhold the requisite means or, in some authoritative manner, direct the contrary.' But there need be no resort to force or blood-shed in enforcing the laws: 'The power confided to me will be used to hold, occupy and possess the property and places belonging to the Government and to collect the duties and imposts; but beyond what may be necessary for those objects there will be no invasion – no using of force against, or among the people anywhere.'

A view of the city of Washington in 1861, with the Capitol, and its unfinished dome, in the foreground. (Radio Times Hulton Picture Library)

He rammed home the lesson, as he hoped, to tactical advantage: 'In *your* hands, my dissatisfied fellow countrymen, and not in *mine*, is the momentous issue of civil war. The Government will not assail you. You can have no conflict without yourselves being the aggressors. . . .' And then the immortal peroration: 'I am loath to close. We are not enemies but friends. We must not be enemies. Though passion may have strained, it must not break our bonds of affection. The mystic chords of memory, stretching from every battlefield and patriot grave, to every living heart and hearth-stone all over this broad land will yet swell the chorus of the Union when again touched, as surely they will be, by the better angels of our nature.'

But now he was President, with vast executive powers and responsibilities. Someone once congratulated Sir Winston Churchill during the war on a great speech. 'If speech-making were all that were necessary,' he replied, 'I'd have beaten Hitler long ago.' Lincoln may have felt like that after the inaugural. The wonderful words about the decision resting with the South concealed, though

98

not from him, his own immediate hideous decision as to what to do about Fort Sumter.

The course he in fact took, his first supreme decision as President, was to make certain that only food supplies should be sent in. In other words, he was very careful to refrain from firing the first shot, while just as carefully he refused to recognize the secession. The outcome of his tactics was by this time inevitable. Fort Sumter and the Federal flag were fired upon. The defence could not be sustained for long. The commanding officer and his men were forced to surrender, marching out with the honours of war, on 14 April. So it was, after all, the South who struck the first blow. If war must come, and Lincoln by now faced it unflinchingly, the North could scarcely hope for a better *casus belli*.

At first sight, the disparity between the combatants was striking. Twenty-three states with a population of twenty-two million were eventually arrayed against eleven states whose population of nine million included nearly four million slaves. But the Southerners took pride in what they believed to be their superior military capacity. Certainly they had more than their fair share of the best generals. Since they claimed only the right to go their own way, their policy could be defensive, inspired by the spirit of self-preservation. The North, which was determined to keep them in the Union by force, had to take the offensive and pursue a course of physical aggression. Nothing could satisfy the North except the military subjugation of their opponents. The twenty-three states were by no means solid. The attitude of the border slave states, Kentucky, Missouri, Maryland and Delaware, was crucial. Lincoln, born in Kentucky, is reported to have said : 'I should like to have God on my side, but I must have Kentucky. To lose Kentucky would be nearly the same as to lose the whole game.' In the event, Lincoln played a major part in securing it for the Union, and Missouri too, after heavy fighting. Maryland and Delaware were also retained and West Virginia won over. Throughout the war, he never lost sight of their attitudes and reactions and was compelled to adapt his strategy accordingly. More broadly, it was his endless task to preserve a united North and foster their appetite for the struggle; to build up overwhelming military potential.

Lincoln, who had never held a higher executive position than that of postmaster at New Salem, now took one far-reaching decision after another. On 15 April, the day after the fall of Fort Sumter, he called a Cabinet meeting. He issued a proclamation calling for seventy-five thousand militia for three months' service.

He appealed to all loyal citizens 'to favour, facilitate and aid this effort to maintain the honour, the integrity and the existence of our National Union and the perpetuity of popular government'. He convened a special session of Congress for 4 July, which meant that for nearly three months he would be in sole charge, though no doubt subjected to a great variety of pressures. Douglas, now a very sick man, came to see his old friend and successful rival, to offer all help in his power to save the Union – a fine episode in the story of America's public men. He approved Lincoln's proclamation, but would have called for far more troops. Three months later, after the Bull Run defeat, we shall find Lincoln appealing for five hundred thousand volunteers, not for three months but for three years. Be that as it may, the response to the proclamation of 15 April was terrific throughout the North. But among his opponents the retaliation was just as heartfelt.

On 19 April, Lincoln took a step which must in the long run prove decisive, if it could be persisted in and not disrupted from outside. He declared on that day an economic blockade of the South. The South had no navy at that time, and apart from a few romantic duels, the North maintained a total command at sea. The Southern leaders reckoned that countries like Britain, deprived of cotton, were bound to intervene. This added to their other grounds for confidence, but Lincoln by that immediate step of 19 April had begun to lay the foundations of victory.

Interpreting his constitutional powers to the legal limit and beyond, Lincoln indeed made the basic decisions of the war on his own responsibility; to reinforce Sumter; to suspend Habeas Corpus and to pay no heed to the protests of the Chief Justice; to ask for troops without authority; to start the fighting before he called Congress, so that he could present that body with a war which was already under way and which must be won; to build for the first time in American history a national army. Lincoln behaved, so his critics alleged, as though the Constitution did not exist. 'I conceive', he said, 'that I may, in an emergency, do things on military grounds that cannot constitutionally be done by Congress. I told a committee in 1862 that as Commander-in-Chief of the army and navy, I suppose I have the right to take any measures which may best subdue the enemy.' He certainly assumed wider powers than any previous President. But Professor Cunliffe concludes that, 'In the light of the war powers exercised by twentieth-century Presidents, his conduct seems understandable and even circumspect – except for the umbrella of martial law

KING COTTON BOUND;
Or, The Modern Prometheus.

Punch cartoon on the North's blockade of Southern ports, authorized by Lincoln on 19 April 1861, which effectively stopped the export of cotton with disastrous economic consequences for the South. (Orbis Publishing Co.)

that prompted him to hold several thousand civilians in jail without process.'

But the fruits of all this intrepidity would take time to reveal themselves. One personal disappointment came his way at the outset. General Lee, everywhere regarded as the ablest officer in the United States army, was invited to call on old General Scott, Lincoln's chief military adviser. Scott lectured Lee on his duty, and Lee was made aware what store President Lincoln set on his services. 'After listening to his remarks,' Lee reported, 'I declined the offer he made me, to take command of the army that was to be

OVERLEAF A scene of turmoil in the House of Representatives in April 1861. (Mansell Collection)

101

brought into the field.' He stated as candidly and courteously as he could that, though opposed to secession and deprecating war, 'I could take no part in invasion of the Southern states.' He then rode across the Long Bridge to Virginia, to take charge of the Southern forces, and to earn undying fame as one of the greatest captains in history and one of the noblest of men.

Today, if one meditates in front of the graves and monuments at Gettysburg for example, one asks oneself inevitably what ideals produced such self-sacrifice and faithfulness to death on both sides. Loyalty no doubt was equal and opposite. In Lee's case the provincial patriotism, the loyalty to Virginia, over-rode the wider patriotism, the loyalty to the United States. Unless one grasps that fully, one cannot begin to understand the prolonged, the more than heroic – the quasi-suicidal resistance of the Southern states.

With the secession of Virginia, Washington, the Northern capital, lay on the actual frontier and was for a time in dire peril. The city had no military protection. The troops eagerly awaited did not arrive. Lincoln paced the floor of his study, 'stopped and gazed long and wistfully out of the window down the Potomac in the direction of the expected ships and, unconscious of others present in the room, at length broke out with irrepressible anguish in the repeated exclamation: "Why don't they come! Why don't they come!"' To the wounded soldiers who came to pay their respects, he said bitterly: 'I begin to believe that there is no North. The 7th Regiment [the troops expected] is a myth. Rhode Island is another. You are the only real thing.' But at last, on 25 April, the troops arrived. The capital was saved. But its continued exposure was a gravely complicating factor in Lincoln's strategy throughout the war and one which was always on his mind. Richmond, the Southern capital, was less than a hundred miles away to the south-west, but if the North took Richmond, nothing decisive would happen. If Washington fell, the North might well be forced to abandon the struggle.

Lincoln called for a great increase of the army and navy, but the Northern populace were in no mood to wait. 'On to Richmond!' was the cry. The elderly Scott favoured a policy of caution, but Lincoln reckoned that delay might prove fatal to the Northern enthusiasm. He ordered General Irvin McDowell to move on without delay. McDowell begged for a little time to organize his 'green troops'. 'You are green, it is true,' replied Lincoln, 'but they are green also. You are all green alike.' So McDowell thrust

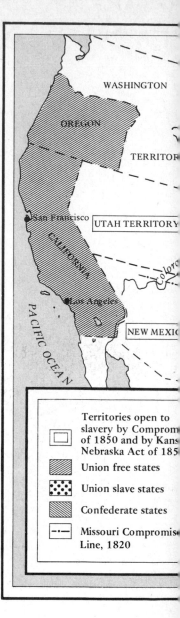

Territories open to slavery by Comprom[ise] of 1850 and by Kans[as]-Nebraska Act of 185[4]

Union free states

Union slave states

Confederate states

Missouri Compromis[e] Line, 1820

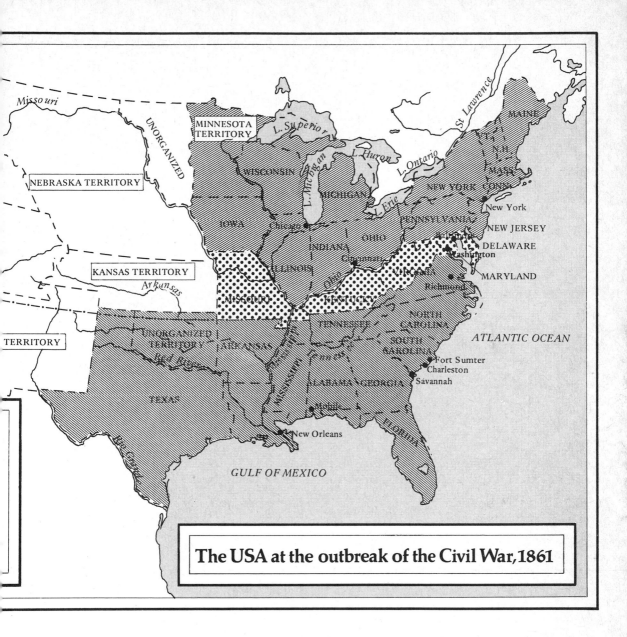

The USA at the outbreak of the Civil War, 1861

bravely forward on 16 July. On 21 July the two armies met. Thirty-five thousand Union troops crossed Bull Run to attack the Confederates under General Beauregard and at first gained ground, but General Johnston from the Shenandoah Valley brilliantly reinforced Beauregard by a surprise movement. The Confederates counter-attacked and the Northern troops broke.

When Lincoln reached the War Department, a telegram informed

OPPOSITE Northern
recruiting poster. At first
Lincoln and his generals
underestimated the number
of troops needed to bring
the war to a successful
conclusion, but they soon
realized what a long and
bitter struggle it would be.
(John Frost Historical
Newspaper Collection)

RIGHT A New York state
private of Zouaves. Their
uniforms were based on the
French colonial uniforms.
(Anne S. K. Brown Military
Collection)

BELOW LEFT AND RIGHT
Uniforms of the Confederate
Army from *Harper's Weekly*.
(British Museum)

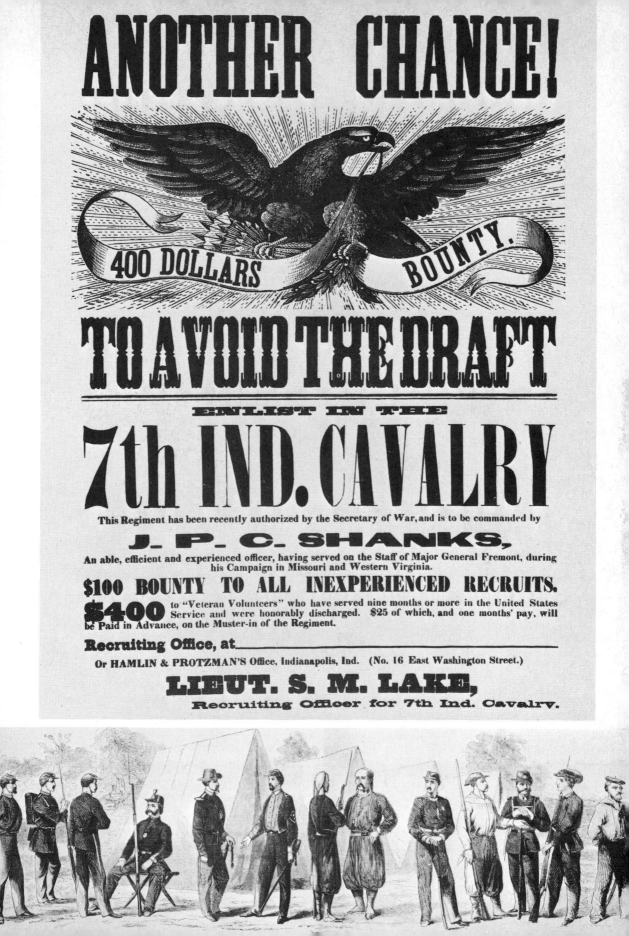

General Irvin McDowell, Union commander at the first battle of Bull Run where the North suffered its first great defeat. After Bull Run, McClellan was called to Washington to reorganize the army. (National Archives)

him 'General McDowell's army in full retreat throughout Centreville. The day is lost. Save Washington and the remnants of this army. The routed troops will not re-form.' An old friend of Lincoln's recalled that when he in his turn reached the War Department, he found a large crowd all in a state of ignorance and confusion. Lincoln came out, making for the White House and at first informed his old friend that he could tell him nothing. 'These war fellows', he said complainingly, 'are very strict with me; I must obey them, I suppose, until I get the hang of things.' 'But Mr President,' insisted his old friend, 'if you cannot tell me the news you can at least indicate its nature, that is whether good or bad.' Grasping his friend's arm, he leaned over, placed his face near his ear and said 'in a shrill, but subdued voice, "It's damn bad!"' It was the first time his friend had ever heard him use profane language.

In conference with Lincoln, General Scott said to him: 'I am the greatest coward in America. I deserve removal because I did not stand up when my army was not in condition for fighting and resist it to the last.' Lincoln replied: 'Your conversation seems to imply that I forced you to fight this battle.' This was just about the truth, but Scott avoided saying so. 'I have never served a President who had been kinder to me than you have been.' The agony of Lincoln seemed to be widely understood, then and later. Walt

108

Whitman wrote: 'If there was nothing else of Abraham Lincoln for history to stamp him with, it is enough to send him with his wreath to the memory of all future time that he endured that hour, that day, bitterer than gall; indeed a crucifixion day; that it did not conquer him, that he unflinchingly stemmed it and resolved to lift himself and the Union out of it.'

The next day Lincoln called General George B. McClellan to Washington and entrusted him with its defence. (McDowell later appeared before a Court of Inquiry. Noah Brooks referred to his full face and commanding military figure: his manner was dignified, decisive and 'at times almost solemn'.) The rout of Bull Run lulled the South into undue self-confidence, but roused the North to furious resolution. It was followed by what has been called 'The Second Uprising'. Congress authorized the enlistment of five hundred thousand three-year volunteers and again recruits poured in. McClellan, a splendid organizer, soon built the Army of the Potomac into a powerful force, much better trained and disciplined.

Northern newspaper report of the Union defeat at Bull Run. This defeat came as a terrible shock to the North. (John Frost Historical Newspaper Collection)

Lincoln's appointment of McClellan to command the Army of the Potomac was to prove fateful. Lincoln moved him up and down, as we shall see. He made him Commander-in-Chief when the aged Scott retired in November. He withdrew that part of his role, without telling him in advance, when McClellan set off in March 1862 on his vast outflanking assault on Richmond. When that had gone astray, Lincoln transferred his army away from him. When Pope, who had supplanted McClellan, had been crushed, Lincoln gave back McClellan his army and Pope's as well and called on him to save Washington. In November 1862, Lincoln dismissed him finally. His attitude to McClellan does not read well in Lincoln's biography. To understand it is, however, to forgive a great deal, though not perhaps everything.

McClellan was thirty-five years old, with an excellent record in the Mexican War as a railway administrator, and already in the Civil War in Western Virginia, which he had done much to save for the Union. Undeniably, he appears in his memoirs as vain and egotistic, but one cannot doubt that he possessed magnetism, or that he was beloved by his men, even in disaster. When he was reinstated after the fall of Pope, his soldiers embraced and kissed his horse's legs. He stood as Democratic candidate for the Presidency against Lincoln in 1864. Though well beaten in the end, he seemed to Lincoln at one moment the likely victor. His abilities as a trainer and organizer were and are unquestionable. Lee reckoned that he was far the ablest general who opposed him, which puts him, on that showing, well above Grant. The fact that Lee was defeated in the end by Grant, and must be thought to have had the better of McClellan, does not prove him wrong.

But McClellan suffered from two major disqualifications which impaired him and, in the end, destroyed his relationship with Lincoln. Churchill is, on the whole, favourable to him: 'Ill treatment was meted out to General McClellan by the Washington politicians and Cabinet, with the cautious pliant General Halleck as their tool.' (Halleck was appointed chief military adviser in July 1862.) 'For this,' he goes on, 'Lincoln cannot escape blame.' But he seeks to adjust the balance fairly. Lincoln 'wanted an aggressive General, who would energetically seek out Lee and beat him. McClellan, for all his qualities of leadership, lacked the final ounces of fighting spirit. Lincoln, with his shrewd judgment of men, knew this.' But McClellan had harsher critics than Lincoln to deal with. He was subjected to intense pressure, notably from a committee of Congress set up in the autumn of 1861. It was

110

dominated by radical Republicans, vehemently opposed to McClellan, partly because he was a prominent Democrat, and partly because they demanded at all costs immediate and aggressive action. They were not at all sure that McClellan's heart was in the war that they believed in. Whether McClellan was or was not an outstanding General, he was going to have a difficult time in any case.

But he brought much additional trouble on himself through his own weaknesses, including vanity. The lack of communication between him and Lincoln has been commented on endlessly. One can allocate the blame as one chooses, but a dispassionate judge like General Sir Frederick Maurice in his *Statesmen and Soldiers of the Civil War* finds that the main fault was McClellan's. Many soldiers are contemptuous of politicians, but McClellan, who was, after all, himself to be a Presidential candidate within three years, is found writing to his wife in autumn 1861: 'I am daily more disgusted with this administration, perfectly sick of it. There are some of the greatest geese in the Cabinet I have ever seen – enough to tax the patience of Job. . . . It is sickening in the extreme, and makes me feel heavy at heart, when I see the weakness and unfitness of the poor beings who control the destinies of this great country.'

Lincoln at this time was studying the military art and borrowing military treatises from the library at Congress. He used to visit McClellan's headquarters to discuss common problems with him. One can understand that a professional soldier might be bored, but it was certainly unwise to show it. Yet Lincoln was, as always, wonderfully tolerant and unresentful. On one occasion, he, Seward and Hay dropped in on McClellan. After an hour's wait, McClellan came in. He was told of the visitors, but went directly upstairs. A half-hour passed; a servant sent to remind him of his company returned to inform them that the General had gone to bed. The President refused to take offence. 'I will hold McClellan's horse', he said later, 'if he will only bring us success.' From then on, however, he used to summon McClellan to the White House if he wished to talk to him, which was obviously more sensible.

Lack of communication was especially pernicious in the case of Lincoln and McClellan. Lincoln, as supreme war leader, had to take account of so many wide political considerations, above all the protection of Washington, which lay outside the strict requirements of the military text book. But McClellan was prevented from understanding these by his own refusal to go half way to

MAJ. GEN. GEO. B. McCLELLAN, U.S.A.

Major-General George B. McClellan, who was appointed General-in-Chief of the US Army when Scott retired. Lincoln, frequently frustrated by McClellan's refusal to take decisive action, once said, 'If General McClellan does not want to use the army for some days, I should like to borrow it and see if it cannot be made to do something.' (Courtesy of the New-York Historical Society)

enter Lincoln's mind. His employment of detectives from a private agency to obtain information about the enemy led him to over-estimate their numbers grossly.

In late December, McClellan was laid up for several weeks with typhus. Lincoln called at his house, but was not allowed to see him. He had little idea of what McClellan was planning. The committee of Congress visited Lincoln on 6 January and launched a vicious attack on McClellan. Why would he not fight? Did he have secret leanings towards the South? Did he favour slavery? Did he see himself emerging as some kind of dictator? Lincoln held them at bay as best he could, but next day he groaned to the Quartermaster-General: 'What shall I do? The people are impatient; Chase has no

112

money and tells me he can raise no more; the General of the army has typhoid fever. The bottom is out of the tub. What shall I do?' A friend, calling on him about this time, recorded: 'He told me he was thinking of taking the field himself, and suggested several plans of operation. Mercifully he refrained from going as far as this.' It can be argued, however, that more clearly than most of his generals, he saw that the North's great hope of victory lay in sustained co-ordinated attacks, making the fullest use of its superior man-power and economic resources. But it was more than two years later before he found a general, Grant, who could act with him in complete partnership and proper allocation of functions.

In the West, the top priority obviously attached to obtaining control of the whole Mississippi and splitting the Confederacy into two. Little progress had been made in this direction by the end of 1861. Lincoln had chosen, not wisely as it turned out, John C. Frémont, Republican Presidential candidate in 1856, to command the Union forces in the West. Missouri was being ravaged by Confederate guerillas. Frémont announced martial law and the confiscation of the property of all the persons in Missouri who had taken up arms against the Government, including the emancipation of their slaves. Lincoln insisted that the edict be modified. Frémont refused; his determined wife took his answer to the President and asked when he could see her. The reply came back: 'Now, at once. A. Lincoln.' It was almost midnight. Mrs Frémont warned Lincoln that he had better be careful. He might find her husband coming out against him. Lincoln did not give in to that kind of threat. 'It is ordered', he announced, 'that the said proclamation be modified so as to conform to the act of Congress' – in other words, to judicial process. Lincoln was violently abused by anti-slavery Republicans. But Lincoln soon had further grounds for concluding that Frémont must go. Investigators revealed total ineptitude and some contact with criminal elements. Lincoln dismissed him from his command, again encountering vehement abuse. 'Where are you, Thaddeus Stevens?' asked the anti-slavery radicals in Congress, 'that you let the hounds run down your friend Frémont?' But Lincoln pulled through and early in the next year the threat to Missouri was finally disposed of.

At a moment when Lincoln needed every atom of strength and self-confidence, he was smitten where it hurt him most. Mary Lincoln had already made a number of enemies during her time in the White House. The White House itself had badly needed refurbishing. $20,000 was voted by Congress for the purpose, but

Mary Lincoln over-spent the appropriation by $7,000 and
lavished money on her own clothes. She entertained in a style
that was considered by many to be unsuitable in wartime. Her
remarks about her husband's colleagues presumably got round to
them, including the reference to Seward as 'a dirty abolitionist
sneak'. Her brothers and stepbrothers were fighting on the
Confederate side. The three brothers were killed, one by one, in
the Confederate army. But she also had numerous relatives
fighting for the Union. To the aristocratic clique of wealthy
residents in Washington, with their Southern Democratic
sympathies, she was regarded, coming from a high-class family
in Kentucky, as a traitor to her class. Republican women, on the
other hand, called her 'two-thirds slavery and one-third secesh'
(pro secession). There came a terrible day when Lincoln appeared
unaccompanied before the Senate Committee to defend his wife
against charges of conspiring with the South. He spoke for two
minutes and left. The Committee dropped its charges and adjourned.

But there were those who were disgusted with these vindictive
attacks and who were well aware of her intense loyalty to the
Northern cause. Her support for her husband would, in any case,
have been absolute. Moreover, partly through her friendship
with her coloured seamstress, Elizabeth Keckley, a former slave,
she had acquired an exceptionally humane approach to the
colour question and become an even more severe enemy of
slavery than her husband. One experienced journalist wrote:
'Since the time Mrs Madison presided at the White House, it has
not been graced by a lady so well fitted by nature and by education
to dispense its hospitalities as is Mrs Lincoln. Her hospitality is
only equalled by her charity, and her graceful deportment by her
goodness of heart.' Everyone fell for the beloved children –
eight-year-old Tad and eleven-year-old Willie – who rushed
hither and thither with no sense of pomp or protocol.

One evening at a reception early in 1862, Lincoln and Mary
Lincoln were welcoming their guests, while upstairs Willie lay
sick in bed with fever. Both parents were equally anxious and
showed it in their respective ways. Mrs Lincoln entered, dressed
in the height of fashion, with a low-cut dress and a long train.
Lincoln had remained very proud of Mary's appearance. At one
reception he had turned to a woman beside him and said with
evident satisfaction: 'My wife is as handsome as when she was a
girl, and I, a poor nobody then, fell in love with her; and what is
more, I have never fallen out.' But this time, he concealed his fears

114

with the remark: 'Whew! Our cat has a long tail tonight.' And he added: 'Mother, it is my opinion if some of the tail were nearer the head, it would be in better style.'

Willie grew worse. Lincoln and Mary Lincoln visited his room incessantly, but ever more hopelessly. At five o'clock one afternoon, the President's secretary, Nicolay, found Lincoln standing before him. The President's voice choked as he said: 'Well, Nicolay, my boy is gone; he is actually gone.' He burst into tears and went to his office. Mrs Lincoln became hysterical and seemed unable to recover her balance. One day, Lincoln gently led her to a window, put his arm about her waist and, pointing to the asylum in the distance, pleaded: 'Mother, try and control your grief or it will drive you mad and we will have to send you there.' By the end of May, she could write, 'When I think over his short but happy childhood, how much comfort he always was to me, when I can bring myself to realize that he has indeed passed away, my question to myself is: can life be endured?' But her religious faith, supplemented for a time by an interest in spiritualism, came to her rescue. In the letter quoted, she says that 'Dear little Taddy, though equally afflicted, bears up and teaches us a lesson in enduring the stroke to which we must submit.' The conviction that Lincoln truly needed her, braced her afresh. His tenderness and understanding were unlimited. Some strengthening of his own religious convictions is apparent from this time onwards, though the process was to go much further.

The attitude of foreign powers to the Confederate States was of the utmost concern to Lincoln's administration, especially at the beginning. British historians usually claim that the British attitude remained correct throughout. It is admitted that the sympathy of the governing classes inclined towards the South under the influence of social contacts, while radical leaders and the working classes sympathized with the North in spite of the unemployment resulting in Lancashire from the blockade and the cessation of cotton exports. Lord Palmerston, the Prime Minister, and Lord John Russell, the Foreign Secretary, represented on the whole the large middle party. But they were deeply perplexed, to quote the *Cambridge Modern History*, 'by the oft repeated refusal of the official leaders of the North to admit that their fight was being waged against slavery'. Lincoln and Seward, whatever their personal feelings, could never for a moment forget the necessity of retaining the four slave states on the side of the Union. Each

116

country was very fortunate in its ambassador, Lord Lyons in Washington, Charles Francis Adams in London, sent there in May 1861 by Lincoln.

As early as February 1861, before Lincoln's inauguration, President Buchanan had instructed American ministers abroad to make sure that foreign countries refused to give diplomatic recognition to Confederate representatives. The British reply was considered far from helpful. When Lincoln proclaimed a blockade in April 1861, the British Government recognized the Confederate Government as belligerents – at international law it would seem an inevitable step, but in Federal eyes a further example of British antagonism.

The near fatal happening, however, of 1861, was the episode of the two Confederate agents despatched by their government to France and Britain, who had forcibly been taken off a British ship called the *Trent* by the Federal authorities – to the immense delight of the Northern population. When the news eventually reached Britain, the national fury was unrestrained. One of the American Ambassador's sons wrote to his brother in the United States: 'This nation means to make war; do not doubt it.' Palmerston and Russell penned a despatch which would almost certainly have produced hostilities. Prince Albert, though mortally ill, helped Queen Victoria to insist on its being modified. Even so, the American Cabinet were faced with what could only look like surrender. Lincoln had come to doubt the legal strength of the American argument, but he did not capitulate easily. The American Cabinet argued from ten o'clock in the morning until two o'clock in the afternoon on Christmas Day, but it was not until the following morning that agreement was reached. According to a first-hand account, 'there was great reluctance on the part of some of the members of the Cabinet – and even the President himself – to acknowledge' the reality of the situation. But Lincoln had earlier cautioned Seward 'One war at a time'. The Confederates were released. Other awkward moments in Anglo-American relations were to arise during the war, but the worst one had been surmounted.

Later on, the '*Alabama* Case' was to cause intense friction; its aftermath dragged on for years. In July 1862 the vessel *Alabama* built by Messrs Lairds at Birkenhead was allowed, in spite of an American warning, to make her way to the Azores, where she received armament brought from Liverpool in two British ships. After a most destructive career on the Confederate side, she was

ultimately sunk on 19 June 1864. Heated and prolonged arguments followed; eventually the matter was referred to arbitration by the British and American governments. The court found that Great Britain was legally responsible for the depredations of the *Alabama* and of another ship, the *Florida*, and other items. The damages were fixed at $15,500,000 in gold. It was obviously a highly regrettable business but, unlike the *Trent* case, not one which brought the two countries to the verge of hostilities.

5 Pain and Difficulty 1862

IN A MILITARY SENSE, the Western theatre was likely to prove decisive if the war continued long enough. But the events in the East, with the respective capitals less than a hundred miles apart, were politically dominant. In 1862, the Northern forces fared much better in the former than in the latter area.

In the West there now emerges the figure of Ulysses Grant, destined to do more than anyone except Lincoln to win the war for the North. Lincoln, as we shall see, had a tremendous opinion of Grant, but said of him on one occasion: 'I don't know what to make of Grant, he's such a quiet little fellow.' Agar supplies a vivid impression: 'Grant was five feet eight inches and slightly stooped. He had cold blue eyes and a big jaw hidden behind a scrubby, messy light brown beard which went well with his scrubby, messy uniform.' He weighed about 140 pounds. No one ever achieved such positions of glory with such an unimpressive preceding record. His father owned a farm and a tannery; he himself passed through the United States Military Academy completely undistinguished, except as a horseman. He served efficiently in the Mexican War which later he deplored for ethical reasons. Heavy drinking was already his weakness; in due course he drank himself out of the army. During the next seven years he failed in farming and in selling real estate. When the war came, he was a minor unsuccessful clerk. He did not like war or soldiering. Nor did he have any feelings about slavery one way or the other. He wrote in 1862: 'I have no hobby of my own in regard to the Negro either to effect his freedom or to continue his bondage.' The cause of abolition, therefore, made no appeal to him. Scott Fitzgerald, in *Tender is the Night*, says of his declining hero, Dick Diver, that he awaited like Grant his intricate destiny. No one in 1862, however clairvoyant, could possibly have foreseen that Grant would go down to history as one of the greatest of generals, if admittedly a crude practitioner. Later, he was to become President of the United States – a most unhappy anti-climax.

With the war he returned to the army and soon became a Brigadier-General with no little help from Lincoln, informed about him by a local Congressman. In February he captured the two key positions of Fort Henry on the Tennessee River and Fort Donelson on the Cumberland. On the second occasion he captured almost fourteen thousand prisoners, replying to a request for terms: 'No terms except unconditional and immediate surrender can be accepted. I propose to move immediately upon your works.' The North, short of heroes, was delighted with the

emergence of 'unconditional surrender' Grant. Lincoln was particularly pleased that the young man from his own part of the country had proved so valiant and from that moment took a special interest in Grant. Then, however, Grant suffered a new setback which might have proved fatal. The battle of Shiloh, the most bloodthirsty so far of the war, ended officially as a draw, but Grant had been caught napping and the losses were shocking. Stories of Grant's drinking were revived. Much pressure was brought on Lincoln to discard him, as one who urged this course on the President recalled: 'Lincoln remained silent for what seemed a very long time. He then gathered himself up in his chair and said in a tone of earnestness that I shall never forget: "I can't spare

this man – he fights."' In his mind the contrast with McClellan was obvious.

The North made further gains in the West before their spring offensive ended. Corinth and Memphis were captured. The Mississippi was cleared down to Pittsburg and at the mouth of the river, New Orleans fell into their hands – a major gain. The Southern army escaped and later in the year launched a vigorous counter-offensive without much progress on balance. Grant settled down to besiege Vicksburg. For long months nothing eventuated. In the West it had been, on the whole, a good year for the North.

In the East, the opposite was true and more so. Things could

hardly have been worse – at least, so it seemed to the general public. A line from Siegfried Sassoon's poem: 'And speed glum heroes up the line to death' has a certain bearing on Lincoln's problem in early 1862, though no one could question McClellan's physical courage, let alone that of his troops. Lincoln now took an extraordinary course. On 27 January 1862 he issued the General War Order No. 1, commanding a concerted advance of all the armies on or before 22 February. Four days later a special War Order directed the Army of the Potomac to begin an advance on Richmond by way of Manassas Junction on or before the same date. McClellan asked leave to file objections and produced his own plan. This would involve transporting a large army by sea to a point on the coast from which it could come at Richmond from the side. 'No one', says Churchill, 'can asperse the principle of this conception. It utilized all the forces of the Union Government; it turned the flank of all the Confederate positions between Washington and Richmond; it struck at the forehead of the Confederacy.'

Its details were substantially modified on examination. Fortress Monroe, at the tip of the peninsula between York and James Rivers, was held by the Union and was finally chosen as a safe landing-place. But Lincoln disliked the plan from the first for an understandable and, it must still seem to us, an excellent reason. It would uncover Washington. It would lay it open to Confederate attack at any moment unless so many troops were retained to defend it that McClellan was fatally weakened. This in the end was very much what happened. But before that result was reached, there were to be many frantic arguments on the top level, much hectic scurrying backwards and forwards, and many brave men were to be slaughtered. In retrospect Lincoln was right to feel in his bones that the plan would not work out. Where he was wrong was in allowing it to go forward under a general in whom he had no deep confidence. It is easy to see and say this now.

A lot of hard bargaining took place as to how many troops were to be retained for the defence of Washington. Lincoln felt, with some reason, that here he had been misled by McClellan. He soon discovered that McClellan had left behind only nineteen thousand untrained troops, instead of two to three times that number, as Lincoln had expected. McDowell's corps of thirty-five thousand men was held back by Lincoln from McClellan, in order to cover Washington.

Throughout the peninsular campaign of McClellan in 1862, the

The American Civil

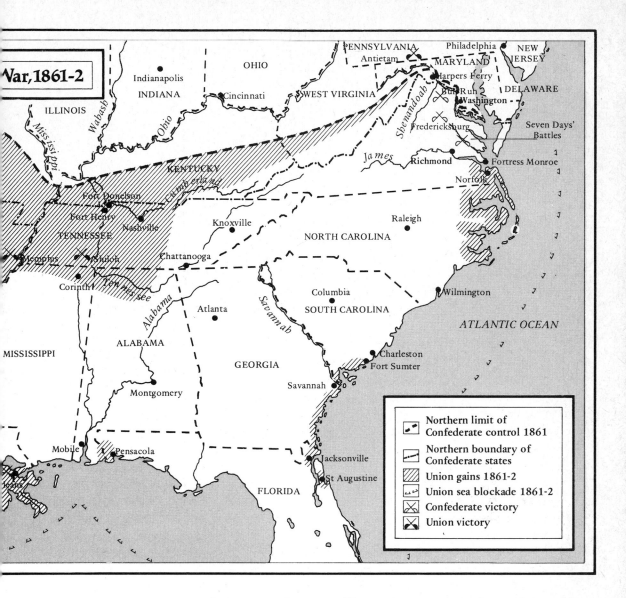

War, 1861-2

Legend:
- Northern limit of Confederate control 1861
- Northern boundary of Confederate states
- Union gains 1861-2
- Union sea blockade 1861-2
- Confederate victory
- Union victory

disposition of McDowell's corps was an acute bone of contention. On three separate occasions, the diversionary operations of Stonewall Jackson in the Shenandoah Valley to the west of Washington caused McDowell's corps to be withheld from McClellan. Throughout the campaign, it has been justly observed that Lee worked on Lincoln's anxiety for the safety of Washington to frustrate the threatened concentration against Richmond. But Lincoln's anxiety was not irrational or neurotic. It was all too well justified. Given the wonderful skill of Lee and Stonewall

Union supply base at Cumberland Landing on the Pamunkey River, Virginia, during McClellan's Peninsular Campaign of 1862. (Library of Congress)

Jackson, his brilliant and heroic lieutenant, a diversionary attack which left Washington uncovered was not likely to succeed.

McClellan and his army embarked on 17 March, disembarking down the coast a month later. With McClellan physically out of touch, Lincoln had some excuse for relieving him of his additional responsibilities as Commander-in-Chief, though the failure to inform him in advance was unfortunate. It is generally asserted however, not least by Sir Winston Churchill, that Lincoln made a serious mistake in not appointing a new Commander-in-Chief, but in taking on the responsibility himself in conjunction with Edwin Stanton. The latter had supplanted Cameron and began in favour of McClellan, but soon turned violently against him. In July, Lincoln brought in General Halleck from the West as his military adviser. No one seems to have a good word for him.

McClellan occupied the peninsula for four and a half months – from the beginning of April till the middle of August; at one point his outposts were only a few miles from the Southern capital. In mid-May he was strongly attacked by General Johnston in the battle of Fair Oaks or Seven Pines. The affair was inconclusive but Johnston was seriously wounded and replaced by the immortal General Lee. From 26 June to 2 July raged the far-famed battles of the Seven Days. McClellan's generalship was skilful but negative throughout. The South lost twenty thousand to the seventeen thousand of the North, who could spare them better, but the battles

128

of the Seven Days were hailed everywhere as a major defeat for the Federal Army. McClellan was thrown back from Richmond; his great expedition had failed.

Our concern here is with Abraham Lincoln and not with military history as such. We must look through his eyes during this harrowing period. Lincoln repeatedly pressed McClellan to take the initiative:

Once more [he concluded], let me tell you it is indispensable to *you* that you strike a blow. *I* am powerless to help this. You will do me the justice to remember I always insisted that going down the Bay in search of a field, instead of fighting at or near Manassas was only shifting and not surmounting a difficulty – that we would find the same enemy and the same, or equal entrenchments, at either place. The country will not fail to note – is now noting – that the present hesitation to move upon an entrenched enemy is but the story of the Manassas repeated.

In May Lincoln, Stanton and Chase visited the front and helped, it seems, to suggest a suitable landing point for the capture of Norfolk, which immediately surrendered with six thousand men. The defenders blew up the frigate *Merrimac* which had been refurbished by the Confederates in astonishing fashion. It was given steam engines and a low penthouse of teak with two layers of railway-iron providing an ironclad shelter. A heavy metal ram was fastened to the prow and a battery of ten seven-inch rifle guns was mounted. Her first appearance on 8 March had spread

The battle of Malvern Hill on 1 July 1862, the climax of the Seven Days' battles and of the Peninsular Campaign. Although on this occasion McClellan won a victory, instead of following it up he withdrew to Harrison's Landing on the James River. Pencil sketch by Alfred R. Waud. (Library of Congress)

LEFT Stonewall Jackson, the most able of Lee's generals; portrait by J. A. Elder. (In the W. W. Corcoran Collection of the Corcoran Gallery of Art)

OPPOSITE Robert E. Lee, perhaps the greatest and certainly the best-loved general of the Civil War. He was offered the post of Commander-in-Chief of the Union Army, but when he realized that it would mean fighting against his native state, Virginia, he refused the post and joined the Confederate states. (Courtesy Virginia Historical Society)

immediate alarm and despondency. She smashed up the Federal ships *Cumberland* and *Congress* and, although for a long time under the fire of at least a hundred guns, her armour was hardly damaged. Mercifully for the North, a *Deus ex machina* appeared the next morning in the form of the *Monitor*. She carried only two guns but they were eleven-inch. She had a turtle-deck protected almost flush with the waterline. For six hours, what Sir Winston Churchill calls 'these iron-clad monsters' battered each other, with hardly any injury, cancelling each other out. As soon as the

130

news reached Europe, it was realized that all the war fleets of the world were obsolete. The British Admiralty by an intense effort in the course of a few years reconstructed the Royal Navy, so as to meet the altered conditions. But from the point of view of the Confederates the *Merrimac* had shot her bolt. When Norfolk was evacuated, it was found impossible to take her up the James River for the defence of Richmond. On the orders of her Captain, she was burned and sunk.

Lincoln returned to Washington with an optimistic report. But now Jackson was on the move again in the Shenandoah Valley and for the next few weeks his hands were over full. Sir Frederick Maurice, who is more favourable to Lincoln than to McClellan, is very severe on Lincoln and Stanton during this period:

Confronted with what they believed to be a great national emergency and having no machinery to deal with it, Lincoln and Stanton took it upon themselves to devise manœuvres and combinations of troops which had very little relation to the facts of the situation, and to issue military orders which were as bad of their kind as they well could be. The effect of these orders has been well summarised by Henderson as causing 175,000 men to be absolutely paralysed by sixteen thousand. Lee in Richmond could hardly, if he had the power for twenty-four hours of issuing orders to the Federal forces, have devised any arrangements more exactly suited to his needs.

The Seven Days' battles, from 26 June to 2 July, came and went. The Northern army were farther back than previously. Gloom in Washington was overwhelming. The lines on Lincoln's face deepened, but he was as inflexible as ever. The affection felt for him among ordinary soldiers remained profound. When he and Stanton reviewed the troops, one soldier wrote:

I have seldom witnessed a more ludicrous sight than our worthy Chief Magistrate presented on horseback yesterday. It did seem as though every moment the President's legs would become entangled with those of the horse he rode and both came down together, while his army were apparently subject to similar mishaps ... the removal of his hat before each regiment was also a source of laughter in the style of its execution ... But the boys liked him, in fact his popularity with the army is and has been universal. Most of our rulers and leaders fall into odium, but all have faith in Lincoln. 'When he finds out, they say, it will be stopped.' ... His benign smile as he passed by was a real reflection of his honest, kindly heart, but deeper, under the surface of that marked and not all uncomely face were the signs of care and anxiety. God bless the man and give answer to the prayers for guidance I am sure he offers.

The duel between the Union *Monitor* (left) and the Confederate *Merrimac*, which lasted for six hours and ended in a draw. The battle between these two 'iron-clad monsters' marked a turning-point in naval history – the era of wooden fighting ships was over. (Colonial Williamsburg)

The value of his war leadership could never be assessed solely in terms of his military dispositions.

On 11 July Lincoln appointed General Halleck to command all land forces of the United States, although until the coming of Grant in 1864 it is difficult to feel that the responsibility of Lincoln and Stanton for the higher strategy was much diminished. When Halleck arrived, Lincoln noted 'his stooped posture, flabby cheeks, ample paunch and large head with heavy features and bulging eyes'. Lincoln could only hope that he deserved his military nickname of 'Old Brains'. Brainy or otherwise, Halleck concluded, and Lincoln concurred, that the whole Yorktown

expedition must be called off and the troops brought back. Taking all the political and personal factors into account, the thing had been a mistake from the beginning.

Now the spotlight fell on General Pope, as inclined as McClellan to over-dramatize himself, and a much more disastrous figure. Lincoln had appointed him at the end of June to command all the troops in Virginia and around Washington, with the exception of the Army of the Potomac. Now McClellan's troops were transferred as rapidly as possible to supplement Pope's forces until McClellan had not even his personal escort with him. Lincoln condemned him bitterly at the time for not producing these reinforcements more speedily. Churchill's verdict is unassailable: Lincoln exchanged horses in mid-stream and got a poorer mount.

Pope did not last long. Subjected to one of the greatest of Lee's enveloping movements, through the agency of Jackson, Pope and his army were utterly defeated at the second battle of Manassas and streamed back in disorder to Washington. Lincoln rose to the occasion as few others would have done. He gave McClellan immediate command of all the troops in and around Washington and united under him his old Army of the Potomac which he was

The second battle of Manassas (also known as the second battle of Bull Run), fought from 24–30 August 1862. The Union troops, under the command of General Pope, were once more disastrously defeated by Lee and Jackson. Pope was recalled to Washington and McClellan was again entrusted with command of the army. (Anne S. K. Brown Military Collection)

in the process of losing, and the army of Pope. The Cabinet expressed utter consternation. Only Blair supported the President but Chase came to agree that he had no alternative. 'It is indeed humiliating,' he recorded, 'but prompted, I believe, by a sincere desire to serve the country, and a fear that should he supersede McClellan by any other commander, no advantage would be gained in leadership, but much harm in the disaffection of officers and troops.' Lincoln said of McClellan at this time 'that he had behaved despicably towards Pope. He really wanted him to fail.' But this kind of consideration weighed with him little. He also said of him: 'There was no man in the army who could man these fortifications and lick these troops of ours into shape as well as he.' That was what counted with Lincoln. McClellan accepted his onerous role without conditions and wrote of his task more humbly than usual: 'I will do my best with God's help to perform it.'

Nevertheless, the tables had been turned in the last four months with a vengeance. When Lee had been given command of the Southern forces at the beginning of June, the Federals were within five miles of Richmond. Now the Confederates were within twenty miles of Washington. It is difficult to think that they made the most of their advantage though Lee invaded Maryland and Jackson captured Harpers Ferry with eleven thousand prisoners; Lincoln followed events night after night with painful vigilance. His fatalism took on a more and more religious character. 'The will of God prevails', he wrote. 'In great contests each party claims to act in accordance with the will of God. Both may be and one must be wrong. God cannot be *for* and against the same thing at the same time.' It seemed to him quite possible that God's purpose was something quite different from the purpose of either party and yet the human instrumentalities might be those best adapted to effect His purpose. 'I am almost ready to say that God wills this contest and wills that it shall not end yet. By His mere quiet power on the minds of the contestants, He could have either *saved* or *destroyed* the Union without a human contest. Yet the contest began. And having begun, He could give the final victory to either side any day. Yet the contest proceeds.' By this time he firmly believed that the will of God existed, and that it was his own paramount duty to seek it and carry it out. But he believed also that neither he nor anyone could ever expect to be certain about its precise application. It was enveloped, and always would be, in profound mystery.

The harsh battle of Antietam followed on 17 September,

with cruel losses on both sides. McClellan informed Halleck: 'Our victory was complete. The enemy is driven back into Virginia. Maryland and Pennsylvania are safe.' Lincoln had grown sceptical about that kind of self-congratulation. The battle is usually described as a draw, but it was quite true that Lee had thought it prudent to withdraw into Virginia. Lincoln found it possible to write to a friend: 'I suppose our victory at Antietam will condone my offence at re-appointing McClellan. If the battle had gone against us, poor McClellan and I too would be in a bad row of stumps.' At the same time he wired McClellan: 'God bless you and all with you. Destroy the rebel army if possible.'

A major battle which would be claimed as some sort of victory gave Lincoln the chance he had been waiting for. On 22 September he issued his famous emancipation proclamation. He announced that persons held as slaves 'within areas in rebellion against the United States would be free on or after 1 January 1863'. It is hardly necessary to point out that it was not *this* proclamation which abolished slavery in America. Lincoln did not announce that policy until two years later and it was not finally ratified until some months after his death. At this time (September 1862) he could claim, if he wished, that he was not departing from the principle laid down in replying to Greeley in August. Greeley had accused the President of letting himself be influenced by certain border state politicians who wanted him to forget that 'Slavery is everywhere the inciting cause and sustained base of treason.' He declared that the President was 'strangely and disastrously remiss'. Greeley informed Lincoln that the people of the country 'require of you as the first servant of the Republic that you execute the laws'. Lincoln already had in mind his emancipation proclamation but he answered Greeley without reference to it. 'What I do about slavery I do because it helps to save the Union and what I forbear, I forbear because I do not believe that it would help to save the Union.' In fact he had, for some time, been turning over in his mind the emancipation proposal. He took very seriously his oath to uphold the Constitution which restrained him, in his view, from a drastic approach to abolition. But he believed that measures otherwise unconstitutional might become lawful when the nation was in peril. To use Benjamin Thomas's phrase, 'He must not lose the game with any card unplayed.'

At a Cabinet meeting on 22 July, he had read a draft proclamation freeing all slaves in the rebellious states. He had made up his mind on the question of principle, but he was anxious to have

136

advice on detail. Seward argued impressively that while the principle was acceptable, the timing was unpropitious because of the unfavourable military situation. While things were going so wrong, such an announcement would seem like a cry of desperation: 'The cry would go up – the Government is stretching forth its hands to Ethiopia, instead of Ethiopia stretching forth her hands to the Government.' Lincoln and everyone else agreed. Lincoln decided to hold the document over 'till the moment was right'. The battle of Antietam met his requirement.

The effect abroad of the emancipation proclamation was far-reaching. When the news of the second battle of Manassas reached England, it had seemed at first to Lord John Russell that the failure of the North was certain and he asked Palmerston and his colleagues to consider whether they must not soon recognize the Confederacy and whether mediation in the interests of peace and humanity

Confederate troops crossing the Potomac before the battle of Antietam. It was McClellan's failure to follow up this victory which finally convinced Lincoln that the Union army would never be successful under McClellan's leadership. (Library of Congress)

PROCLAMATION OF EMANCIPATION

BY THE PRESIDENT OF THE UNITED STATES OF AMERICA.

Whereas, On the Twenty-Second day of September, in the year of our Lord One Thousand Eight Hundred and Sixty-Two, a Proclamation was issued by the President of the United States, containing, among other things, the following, to wit:

"That on the First day of January, in the year of our Lord One Thousand Eight Hundred and Sixty-Three, all persons held as Slaves within any State, or designated part of a State, the people whereof shall then be in rebellion against the United States, shall be then, thenceforth, and **FOREVER FREE,** and the *Executive Government of the United States,* including the Military and Naval Authorities thereof, *will recognise and maintain the freedom of such persons,* and will do no act or acts to repress such persons, or any of them, in any efforts they may make for their actual freedom.

"That the Executive will, on the First day of January aforesaid, by proclamation, designate the States and parts of States, if any, in which the people thereof respectively shall then be in rebellion against the United States, and the fact that any State, or the people thereof, shall on that day be in good faith represented in the Congress of the United States by members chosen thereto at elections wherein a majority of the qualified voters of such State shall have participated, shall, in the absence of strong countervailing testimony, be deemed conclusive evidence that such State and the people thereof are not then in rebellion against the United States."

Now, therefore, I, ABRAHAM LINCOLN, PRESIDENT OF THE UNITED STATES, by virtue of the power in me vested as **Commander-in-Chief of the Army and Navy of the United States** in time of actual armed rebellion against the authority and government of the United States, and as a fit and necessary war measure for suppressing said rebellion, do, on this First day of January, in the year of our Lord One Thousand Eight Hundred and Sixty-Three, and in accordance with my purpose so to do, publicly proclaim for the full period of one hundred days from the day of the first above-mentioned order, and designate, as the States and parts of States wherein the people thereof respectively are this day in rebellion against the United States, the following, to wit: — **Arkansas, Texas, Louisiana,** (except the Parishes of St. Bernard, Plaquemines, Jefferson, St. John, St. Charles, St. James, Ascension, Assumption, Terre Bonne, La Fourche, St. Mary, St. Martin, and Orleans, including the City of Orleans,) **Mississippi, Alabama, Florida, Georgia, South Carolina, North Carolina, and Virginia,** (except the forty-eight counties designated as West Virginia, and also the counties of Berkeley, Accomac, Northampton, Elizabeth City, York, Princess Ann, and Norfolk, including the cities of Norfolk and Portsmouth,) and which excepted parts are for the present left precisely as if this Proclamation were not issued.

And by virtue of the power and for the purpose aforesaid, I do order and declare that **ALL PERSONS HELD AS SLAVES** within said designated States and parts of States ARE, AND HENCEFORWARD **SHALL BE FREE!** and that the Executive Government of the United States, including the Military and Naval Authorities thereof, will recognize and maintain the freedom of said persons.

And I hereby enjoin upon the people so declared to be free to abstain from all violence, UNLESS IN NECESSARY SELF-DEFENCE; and I recommend to them that in all cases, when allowed, they LABOR FAITHFULLY FOR REASONABLE WAGES.

And I further declare and make known that such persons of suitable condition will be received into the armed service of the United States, to garrison forts, positions, stations, and other places, and to man vessels of all sorts in said service.

And upon this act, sincerely believed to be AN ACT OF JUSTICE, warranted by the Constitution, upon military necessity, I invoke the considerate judgment of mankind and the gracious favor of ALMIGHTY GOD!

In Testimony Whereof, I have hereunto set my name, and caused the seal of the United States to be affixed.

Done at the CITY OF WASHINGTON, this First day of January, in the Year of our Lord One Thousand Eight Hundred and Sixty-Three, and of the Independence of the United States the Eighty Seventh.

[L. S.]

By the President,

William H. Seward

Secretary of State.

A. Lincoln.

J. MAYER & CO. LITH. 4 STATE ST. BOSTON.

might not follow. 'But within two months', says Lord Charnwood, 'all thought of recognizing the Confederacy was completely put aside and an invitation from Louis Napoleon to joint action between England and France had once and for all been rejected.' The battle of Antietam, he reckoned, had contributed something, but the emancipation proclamation vastly more to this fundamental change of attitude. Broadly speaking this must be taken as a correct assessment. One cannot help noticing, however, that it was *after* the proclamation, in fact on 7 October, that Gladstone, Chancellor of the Exchequer, made his celebrated gaffe when he said: 'Jefferson Davis had made a nation' – in other words, the South should be placed on the same footing as the North. Gladstone was in fact repudiated. It is true that as late as 13 June 1863, Gladstone was saying to the House of Commons that 'Public opinion was unanimous that the restoration of the American Union by force was unattainable.' Nevertheless in the long perspective of history, it seems right to treat the emancipation proclamation of 22 September 1862, as a major turning-point in the British attitude towards the American Civil War.

OPPOSITE The proclamation of emancipation signed by Lincoln on 1 January 1863. A few months before, Lincoln had told Horace Greeley, 'What I do about slavery, and the coloured race, I do because I believe it helps to save the Union. . . .' (John Frost Historical Newspaper Collection)

BELOW Lincoln reading the draft of the emancipation proclamation to his Cabinet on 22 July 1862. His Secretary of State, Seward, convinced him that it should be issued at a moment of strength. Five days after the victory at Antietam the preliminary proclamation was published. (Bettmann Archive)

At home in the United States, the immediate benefits were much more questionable. Pressure from the Republican Governors was relieved, but the mid-term election of 1862 went very badly for the Republicans. The Northern Democrats who had supported the war felt betrayed. The legislature of Lincoln's own state resolved that the proclamation was

... a gigantic usurpation, at once converting the war, professedly commenced by the administration for the vindication of the Constitution into a crusade for the sudden unconditional and violent liberation of three million Negro slaves; a result which would not only be a total subversion of the Federal Union but a revolution in the social organization of the Southern states, the immediate and remote, the present and far-reaching

consequences of which to both races cannot be contemplated without the most dismal foreboding of horror and dismay.

Colonel Henderson is surprisingly emphatic about the military benefits. He admits that the army had small sympathy with the coloured race and the political opponents of the President accused him vehemently of unconstitutional action, but he sums up this way: 'Enthusiasm in the cause was fast diminishing when Lincoln, purely on his own initiative, proclaimed emancipation and, investing the war with the dignity of a crusade, inspired the soldier with a new incentive and appealed to a feeling which had not yet been stirred.'

Lincoln still clung to his concept of legality and his desire to

Allegorical painting of the emancipation proclamation by A. A. Lamb. (National Gallery of Art, Washington D.C.; Gift of Edgar William and Bernice Chrysler Garbisch, 1955)

OVERLEAF *Allegory of Freedom* by an unknown artist. (National Gallery of Art, Washington D.C.; Gift of Edgar William and Bernice Chrysler Garbisch)

promote racial harmony, as compared with reckless emancipation.
He became more and more convinced that the white race and
the black race would be better off apart; that in view of inherited
prejudices, it would be best to remove the Negroes from the
country. But he would not coerce them into exile. Their departure
must be voluntary. He invited certain intelligent free coloured
men to discuss the problem with him and pointed to areas in
Central America where black men might be assisted to make a
new start. Certain capitalists were willing to sponsor such a
venture. Later he abandoned the Central American project in
favour of a Negro colony on Isle à Vache, a possession of the
Negro Republic of Haiti. More than four hundred Negroes in fact
were sent there at Government expense before the project failed.
Lincoln reluctantly concluded that colonization was hopeless and
that whites and blacks must learn to live together as free men in
the United States. He came to favour the presence of Negroes in
the army from a double standpoint: it could be vital to the war
effort and at the same time to the self-respect of the Negro. The
preliminary emancipation proclamation had not mentioned the
use of Negro soldiers. The operative proclamation of New Year's
Day 1863 gave them their chance. By the end of the war there were
about 186,000 coloured troops in the Union army.

In September 1862 Lincoln pressed McClellan harder than ever
for aggressive action. He visited Antietam and wrote to him,
stirring him on.

> Are you not over-cautious [he asked] when you assume that you
> cannot do what the enemy is constantly doing? . . . Change positions with
> the enemy and think you not he would break your communications with
> Richmond within the next twenty-four hours? . . . If he should . . . move
> towards Richmond, I would press closely to him and at least try to beat
> him to Richmond on the inside track. . . . If we cannot beat the enemy
> where he now is, we never can, he again being within the entrenchments
> of Richmond.

And again, when McClellan excused himself on the grounds that
his horses were sore-tongued and tired, Lincoln enquired sharply,
'Will you pardon me for asking what the horses of your army have
done since the battle of Antietam that fatigues anything?' However, he sent him a soothing letter afterwards. When he visited
McClellan in October he told him that, says the latter, 'he was the
best General in the country'.

144

But soon political pressures and his own impatience became
overriding. McClellan was a prominent Democrat. For his party,
the emancipation proclamation and what it stood for were a bitter
medicine. It can be argued that Lincoln could no longer afford to
employ as his chief general one who was not only influenced by
politics, but by politics which contradicted his own. He clearly
had great doubts as to whether McClellan really wanted to 'hurt'
the enemy, whatever his putative motive. McClellan had not
brought his army into contact with Lee's by 5 November, and on
that date Lincoln, for good or ill, dismissed him. To the politician
Frank Blair who intervened on McClellan's behalf, Lincoln
answered, 'I said I would remove him if he let Lee's army get
away from him and I must do so. He has got the "slows".'

There was almost a mutiny in the army when McClellan's
dismissal was known. The displaced General behaved with perfect

148

loyalty and tried to ease the path of his successor. This was General Burnside who looked up to McClellan and had no desire to take over the command. It had been offered to him twice before, and he had twice declined, feeling that he was not competent for it. But he was handsome, dashing and brave, and seemed to Lincoln to possess the aggressiveness required. Within a month or so he had been totally routed, trying in a clumsy way to give effect to what he imagined to be Lincoln's desire for action at all costs.

He attacked Lee near the town of Fredericksburg, where the position was really impregnable. Lincoln had given a qualified approval to the plan, but only on the assumption that there would be diversified attacks on several points. These Burnside omitted. In Churchill's phrase, he butted straight at the barrier. The result was utterly disastrous. Before nightfall, the losses of the Union amounted to twelve thousand men. In his tent, Burnside cried hysterically, 'Oh! Oh! those men.' He was with difficulty restrained from leading a suicidal attack against the Confederate entrenchments. His senior officers were bitterly critical. Burnside prepared an order, dismissing some of them, including General Hooker, from the army. He told Lincoln that he must either approve his order or accept his, Burnside's, resignation. Lincoln naturally accepted it.

We have already noted the measure of success achieved by the Union troops in the West during the year just ended. But their progress had been maddeningly slow. The Federals had won control of the Mississippi river, except for 250 miles between Vicksburg and Port Hudson. While this stretch of river remained in the hands of the Confederates, the waterway remained closed to the North, and the South were left with an effective means of communication with the outside world. Grant was making very little progress against Vicksburg, still, overall, there had been movement in the right direction.

In the East, on which all political thoughts were focused, the succession of Northern defeats had been almost continuous. General after general had been reduced, in Henderson's words, 'to the ignominy that awaits a defeated leader'. But, 'Not for a single moment had Lincoln wavered from his purpose.' That, no doubt, is absolutely true of his conduct and will-power. His feelings were another matter. To a friend he confided: 'We are on the brink of destruction. It appears to me the Almighty is against us and I can hardly see a ray of hope.'

6 Gleams of Light 1863

LINCOLN NOW HAD TO CHOOSE yet one more new commander for the Army of the Potomac. His choice fell on Joseph Hooker – 'Fighting Joe'. 'A gay cavalier, alert and confident, overflowing with animal spirits and as cheery as a boy.' Hooker liked to talk and boast and even to intrigue, as just previously in his behaviour to Burnside. He soon began bragging of his perfect plans. 'May God', cried Hooker, 'have mercy on General Lee, for I will have none!' Lincoln, who, presumably, liked the idea of 'Fighting Joe', sighed audibly when he heard this. 'That is the most depressing thing about Hooker, it seems to me that he is over confident.' However, this was now his chosen instrument. He accepted the fact that Hooker had no use for Halleck, nominally the General-in-Chief, and agreed to work things out with him directly.

At the end of a long interview, Lincoln handed him a letter which has rightly been regarded as a classic. 'I have placed you', he wrote, 'at the head of the Army of the Potomac. Of course I have done this on what appeared to me sufficient reasons, and yet I think it best for you to know that there are some things in regard to which I am not quite satisfied with you.' He went on to say that he believed Hooker to be a brave and skilful soldier, who did not mix politics with his profession and who had confidence in himself, all of them valuable assets. Then he came nearer the bone:

You are ambitious which, within reasonable bounds, does good rather than harm. But I think that during General Burnside's command of the army you have taken counsel of your ambition and thwarted him as much as you could, in which you did a great wrong to the country, and to a most meritorious and honourable officer. I have heard in such way as to believe it of your recently saying that both the army and the Government needed a dictator. Of course it was not for this, but in spite of this, that I have given you the command. Only those generals who gain successes can set up dictators. What I now ask of you is military success and I will risk the dictatorship.

He assured him that the Government would support him, as they would support all their commanders, but warned him that the spirit of criticizing the commander, which he had helped to infuse into the army, might turn against him though he, as President, would do all in his power to help him put it down. Then the unforgettable conclusion: 'And now, beware of rashness. Beware of rashness, but with energy and sleepless vigilance go forward and give us victories.' Hooker always carried the President's letter around with him in his pocket, and later showed it in camp to a visiting journalist, with the comment: 'This is just such a letter as

152

a father might write to his son. It is a beautiful letter and although I think he was harder on me than I deserve, I will say that I love the man who wrote it.'

But he was defeated in his first large battle, at Chancellorsville, as comprehensively as had been Pope and Burnside. McClellan had never been routed in this way. The battle provided an extraordinary demonstration of the military art by Lee and Jackson, while the soldiers fought with their habitual courage on both sides. Poor Hooker was never in the same league as his opponents.

At the crucial moment it was arranged for Jackson, with twenty-six thousand men, to march round Hooker's right, starting at 4 am, and attack him, while Lee faced nearly eighty thousand Federals, with seventeen thousand. The stroke was brilliantly successful. As Churchill describes it: 'The soldiers of the Eleventh Federal Corps were eating their supper and playing cards behind their defences when suddenly there burst from the forest at their

General Joseph Hooker, known as 'Fighting Joe', who replaced Burnside as commander of the Army of the Potomac in January 1863. (National Archives)

The Old Westover Mansion by
E. L. Henry; Federal troops
occupy a Southern mansion.
(In the Collection of the
Corcoran Gallery of Art;
Gift of the American Art
Association)

155

The battle of Chancellorsville, fought on 1–5 May 1863, when Hooker and the Union Army were defeated by the Confederates. 'My God! my God; what will the country say?', exclaimed Lincoln when he heard the news. Rejoicing in the South was muted, however, because of the death of Stonewall Jackson, accidentally shot during the battle by one of his own men. (Photo Research International)

backs the Confederate line of battle. In one hour the Eleventh Corps, attacked by superior forces in this battle, although as a whole their army was two to one, was dashed into rout and ruin.' And from that *débâcle* there was no recovery.

The journalist Noah Brooks was with Lincoln as he read the telegram containing the news. His face was 'ashen in line and he was a picture of despair. Clasping his hands behind his back he walked up and down the room saying "My God, my God; what will the country say, what will the country say?" But in public and in his actions, he never faltered.'

Lee now carried out his long-planned invasion of Pennsylvania. Two months after Chancellorsville came Gettysburg. The name is imperishable. To rank among the greatest of battles, there should ideally be high drama, abundant heroism among the troops, superlative generalship and a decisive influence on history. Of these criteria, only the third, the generalship, was lacking. Lincoln in his memorial address referred sublimely and with absolute justice to 'the last full measure of devotion' exhibited by the troops on both sides. The most glorious manifestation of it was the final charge of fifteen thousand Confederates, Pickett's Virginians, Pettigrew's North Carolinians and the very flower of the army. But in Churchill's words: 'Like the Old Guard on the evening of Waterloo, they faced odds and metal beyond the virtue of mortals.' As one stands on the grounds today, one marvels that the charge was ever ordered.

156

Woe to the conquered, but woe also on that day to the victors! General Robert Shenk reported to Lincoln: 'I learn that the suffering at the field near Gettysburg and beyond is terrible; in the want of sufficient medical attendance, food and other help.' The North lost twenty-three thousand out of ninety-three thousand, the South about the same number out of seventy thousand. Lee met the remnants, less than a third of the heroic assailants, as they came back. They would not let him say, but he insisted on saying: 'It is all my fault.' Certainly he had not been at his best.

Perhaps Lee had grown over-confident. After all, he had recently thrashed more or less the same army with the odds much heavier against him. What cannot be gainsaid is that for the first time he was without Jackson, and had no one to compare with him to carry out the wide outflanking movements of which Jackson was such a unique exponent. Moreover, at Gettysburg one of his three corps commanders, Longstreet, obstinately opposed his main tactics and, in the event, did much to undo them. Again, Lee had always depended heavily on his cavalry for the information about the enemy on which his lightning combinations depended. On this occasion he had allowed their commander to take them, not for the first time, on a spectacular ride right round the Federal army. But this time it was fatal. It deprived Lee of his eyes and ears during the critical period.

Can we fairly give Lincoln some of the credit? Hooker would have liked to make straight for Richmond, when Lee invaded Pennsylvania. Lincoln, rightly, one must think, insisted on his following Lee. Shortly before the battle, Hooker demanded reinforcements on pain of resignation. Lincoln and Halleck were glad to take him at his word. General Meade replaced him. 'The damned old goggle-eyed snapping turtle', as the troops called him, was no military genius but he was tough and canny. Neither Meade nor Lee had wished the battle to take place at Gettysburg. It arose from a chance collision in an atmosphere of muddle. But a subordinate commander on the Federal side was quick to take advantage of a valuable position and General Meade's defensive dispositions have been generally approved of. If we are going to hold Lincoln responsible in some measure for the failure of Pope, Burnside and Hooker, we must allow him some credit for the memorable success of Meade.

But Lincoln was not in the mood to bestow congratulations in regard to Gettysburg, though he never failed to recognize the unflinching courage of the soldiers. During the battle he had

Major-General George G. Meade, appointed commander of the Army of the Potomac three days before the battle of Gettysburg. When Meade allowed the enemy to escape after the battle, Lincoln lamented, 'We had them within our grasp. We had only to stretch forth our hands, and they were ours.' (National Archives)

endured even more than the usual strains. At dawn on the last day, 3 July, he was at the War Department as usual. The only information reaching them was an overnight message: 'At this moment the battle is raging as fiercely as ever. The loss has been great on both sides. All our forces have been, and still are in action and we shall be compelled to stand and fight it out.' All day the uncertainty persisted. But by midnight it was possible to believe in victory. The next day came the news of Lee's retreat. The War Department rushed twenty thousand fresh troops to Meade and urged on him a *coup de grâce*. There was no immediate response, but now came glorious news – the best of the war, from another quarter. On 7 July it was learned that Grant had captured Vicksburg. Welles, the Secretary of the Navy, dashed round to tell Lincoln. Lincoln leaped up and threw his arms around the stocky Welles, exclaiming: 'What can we do for the Secretary of the Navy for this glorious intelligence? He is always giving us good news. I cannot in words tell you my joy over this result. It is great, Mr Welles! It is great!' Halleck immediately wired Meade, calling for the destruction of Lee's army. 'If so, the rebellion will be over.'

In the West, the main interest for the first six months of the year had centred on Grant's prolonged attempts to capture Vicksburg and, on the personal plane, on Lincoln's defence of him against venomous criticism. Grant's first attempt had failed in December 1862 and soon he was coming under harsh denigration.

158

He was said to be drinking again. Murat Halstead of the *Cincinnati Commercial* wrote to Chase: 'You do once in a while don't you, say a word to the President, or Stanton, or Halleck, about the conduct of the war? Well now, for God's sake say that Genl. Grant entrusted with our greatest army is a jackass in the original package. He is a poor drunken imbecile. He is a poor stick sober, and he is most of the time more than half drunk, and much of the time idiotically drunk. . . .' Chase sent Halstead's letter to Lincoln, who thereupon despatched a Congressman, a Governor and an Adjutant-General to investigate Grant's conduct. They reported that Grant and his men were in excellent order. When a delegation came to Lincoln to demand Grant's dismissal, he made the characteristic quip: 'If I knew what kind of liquor Grant drinks, I would send a barrel or so to some other generals.' But the attacks on Grant became so persistent and so bitter that Lincoln confided to a secretary: 'I think Grant has hardly a friend left except myself.' Lincoln's dealings with Grant, as opposed to McClellan, demonstrate that if Lincoln really believed in a general, he would support him through thick and thin, whatever the political climate.

The operations by which Grant captured Vicksburg were masterly, though they took time to carry out. During the night of 16 April, his troops were ferried past Vicksburg and landed on the east bank, south of the city. General Pemberton commanded thirty-five thousand troops in Vicksburg. Johnston, in command

Confederate prisoners, from Major-General George E. Pickett's Division, taken during the battle of Gettysburg. After Pickett's famous charge had been repulsed on 3 July, the Confederate army retreated. Drawing by Edwin Forbes. (Library of Congress)

159

of all the Confederate troops in the West, had about the same number near Jackson, the capital of Mississippi. By 25 May, his Chiefs-of-Staff could inform Lincoln that Grant had fought and won five battles in three weeks, capturing Jackson, pushing Johnston away and encircling Pemberton in Vicksburg. At this point Grant went on a terrific spree. Luckily a certain Sylvanus Cadwallader of the *Chicago Times* found him in a drunken condition, undressed him and got him to his cabin. Grant sobered up, but then obtained more liquor. Mounting his horse, he dashed wildly back to camp, scattering all and sundry, luckily unrecognized. Cadwallader, faint but pursuing, managed to get him off to sleep again. When he woke up, Grant 'shrugged his shoulders,

Admiral Porter's fleet
running the Confederate
blockade of the Mississippi
at Vicksburg on 16 April
1863. This opened the way
for Grant's successful siege
of the city, which
surrendered on 4 July.
(Library of Congress)

pulled down his vest and shook himself together as one just risen
from a nap'. To some officers waiting for him suspiciously, he said
'Good-night' in a natural tone and manner, and started to his tent
'as steadily as he ever walked in his life'.

But he delivered the goods. When he captured Vicksburg,
Lincoln sent him a message of congratulation. 'I do not remember
that you and I have ever met personally. I write this now as a
grateful acknowledgment for the almost inestimable service you
have done the country.' He went on to say a further word. When
Grant got below Vicksburg, Lincoln had thought that he should
go down the river and join General Banks. 'When you turned
northwards, I feared it was a mistake. I now wish to make the

161

personal acknowledgment that you were right and I was wrong.'

On 9 July, it was known that Grant had captured thirty-eight thousand prisoners, and that Port Hudson, the last southern stronghold on the Mississippi, had surrendered to General Banks. 'The father of waters', said Lincoln, 'again goes unvexed to the sea.' The double news of Gettysburg and Vicksburg sent the North into ecstasies of joy and relief. Everywhere bells pealed and cannons boomed salutes, but Lincoln remained a worried man. When he learned that Meade had congratulated his army on 'driving the enemy from our soil', he shook his head gloomily. 'This is a dreadful reminiscence of McClellan', he complained. 'It is the same spirit that moved him to claim a great victory because Pennsylvania and Maryland were safe. Will our generals never get that idea out of their heads? The whole country is our soil.' Halleck telegraphed Meade: 'I need hardly tell you that the escape of Lee's army without another battle has created great dissatisfaction in the mind of the President.'

Meade asked to be relieved of his command. Lincoln wrote him a long letter. He was grateful for Meade's magnificent success and sorry to cause him the slightest pain, but he was in such deep distress himself that he could not restrain some expression of it. 'My dear General,' wrote the President, 'I do not believe you appreciate the magnitude of the misfortune involved in Lee's escape. He was within your easy grasp, and to have closed upon him would in connection with our other late successes have won the war. As it is, the war will be prolonged indefinitely. Your golden opportunity is gone and I am distressed immeasurably because of it.' He begged Meade not to consider this a prosecution or persecution of himself, but since Meade had learned that Lincoln was dissatisfied, 'I have thought it best to kindly tell you why.' But it was better and kinder still not to. Lincoln placed the letter in an envelope on which he wrote: 'To General Meade. Never sent or signed.'

In the East, there was no serious fighting after July – a somewhat mystifying fact. In the West, the war was fast and furious, much of it centred round Chattanooga, a big railway junction opening the way to Georgia. Rosecrans, the Federal General, had completely out-manœuvred the Confederate Bragg and captured Chattanooga without fighting. But Bragg, heavily reinforced, defeated Rosecrans at Chickamauga, and bottled him up in Chattanooga, threatening to starve him out. On the night of 20 September, Lincoln was summoned from his sleep to the War

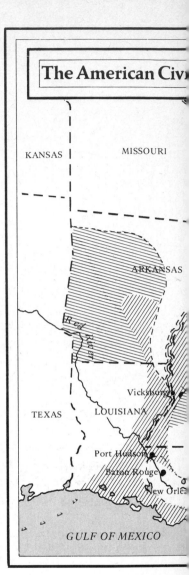

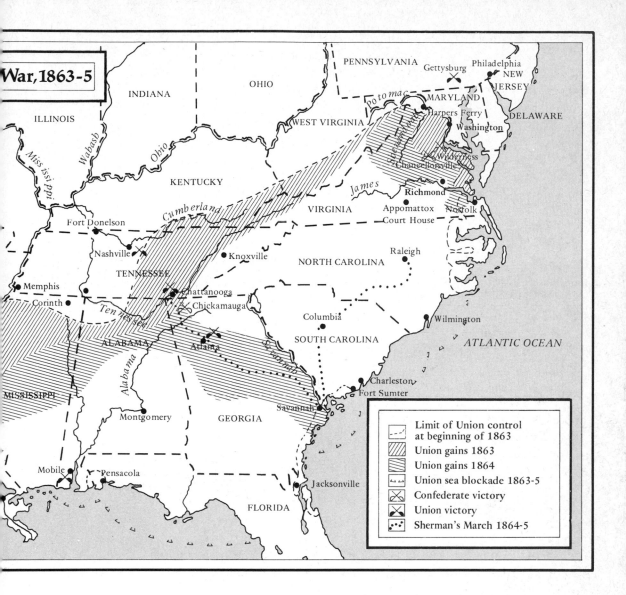

War, 1863-5

PENNSYLVANIA
Gettysburg
Philadelphia
NEW
JERSEY
INDIANA
OHIO
ILLINOIS
MARYLAND
Potomac
Harpers Ferry
DELAWARE
WEST VIRGINIA
Washington
KENTUCKY
Wilderness
Chancellorsville
James
Richmond
Cumberland
VIRGINIA
Appomattox
Norfolk
Fort Donelson
Court House
Nashville
Knoxville
Raleigh
TENNESSEE
NORTH CAROLINA
Memphis
Chattanooga
Corinth
Chickamauga
Tennessee
Columbia
Wilmington
SOUTH CAROLINA
ATLANTIC OCEAN
ALABAMA
Atlanta
MISSISSIPPI
Savannah
Charleston
Fort Sumter
Montgomery
GEORGIA
Mobile
Pensacola
Jacksonville
FLORIDA

	Limit of Union control at beginning of 1863
	Union gains 1863
	Union gains 1864
	Union sea blockade 1863-5
	Confederate victory
	Union victory
	Sherman's March 1864-5

Department and told of the terrible events at Chickamauga. The
collapse of the Union right wing was reminiscent of Bull Run. But
by mid-October, Grant had been installed in charge of the military
division of the Mississippi covering the whole area between the
Alleghenies and the Mississippi, except the territory occupied by
Banks in the south-west. He arrived in Chattanooga on 23
October, carried part of the way after a fall from his horse. Within
a week he had rectified the position, his supply lines were secure
and his troops back on full rations.

Railways

In a conflict fought over vast areas, the speedy movement of troops and supplies was essential to victory. Rail and water communications were thus a vital factor in the Western theatre of the Civil War. To reach the Mississippi and the world beyond by rail, a traveller would have to go through either Chattanooga or Mobile. The capture of these two towns, which would cut the Southern railway system in two, became one of the prime objectives of the Union armies.

BELOW The US Military Construction Corps building a railroad between Fredericksburg and Aquis Creek. (Library of Congress)

RIGHT ABOVE Troops transported by rail on the Nashville and Chattanooga railroad. (Anne S. K. Brown Military Collection)

RIGHT BELOW The smoking
wreck of a Southern railroad
destroyed by Federal raiders.
(National Archives)

A month later he had won a great victory at Chattanooga. A
telegram on 27 November arrived from him: 'I am just in from the
front. The rout of the enemy is most complete. . . .' Lincoln
telegraphed back: 'Understanding that your lodgment at
Chattanooga and Knoxville is now secure, I wish to tender you and
all under your command my more than thanks – my profoundest
gratitude – for the skill, courage and perseverance with which you
and they, over so great difficulties, have effected that important
object. God bless you all.' By the end of the year the Northern
gains looked very solid.

How decisive was Gettysburg? Churchill had no doubts. 'Lee',
he remarks, 'had lost only five guns – and the war.' And a little
later, 'the Confederacy were defeated [after Gettysburg and the
capture of Vicksburg], and the last long phase of the war was one
of subjugation and conquest'. (It lasted twenty-one months.) This
seems to be overstating the matter. It is quite true that never again
would the Confederacy be strong enough to invade the North, nor
impose terms by outright military victory. But we shall find that
late summer 1864 was, from Lincoln's standpoint, in some ways
the worst period of all, in the sense that it became harder and
harder to maintain the united front essential to victory. Without
Lincoln, could it have been done? One takes leave to judge it
unlikely.

After the battle of Gettysburg, thousands of dead soldiers, blue
and grey alike, lay out in the open, united at last – as it has been
well said – in their stillness. Thousands of wooden crosses soon
marked their temporary graves. There was a widespread demand
in Gettysburg and the neighbourhood for a burial-ground
specially dedicated. Seventeen acres of land were bought in the
name of Pennsylvania. The work of removal and reinterment of
the Union dead began at the end of October, but was not completed
for many months. The removal of the Confederate dead and
reinterment in the South was not undertaken until seven years
after the battle. It was decided to organize an impressive ceremony
of dedication. This, after a postponement, took place on 19
November. Edward Everett, one of the country's foremost orators,
was asked to deliver the main address. Lincoln, along with other
high-ranking persons, was invited to the ceremony, but was not
asked to make a speech. It was not thought that the President
'would be able to speak upon such a great and solemn occasion as
that of the Memorial services'. Moreover, the cemetery was not at
that time under the authority of the Federal government. Lincoln,

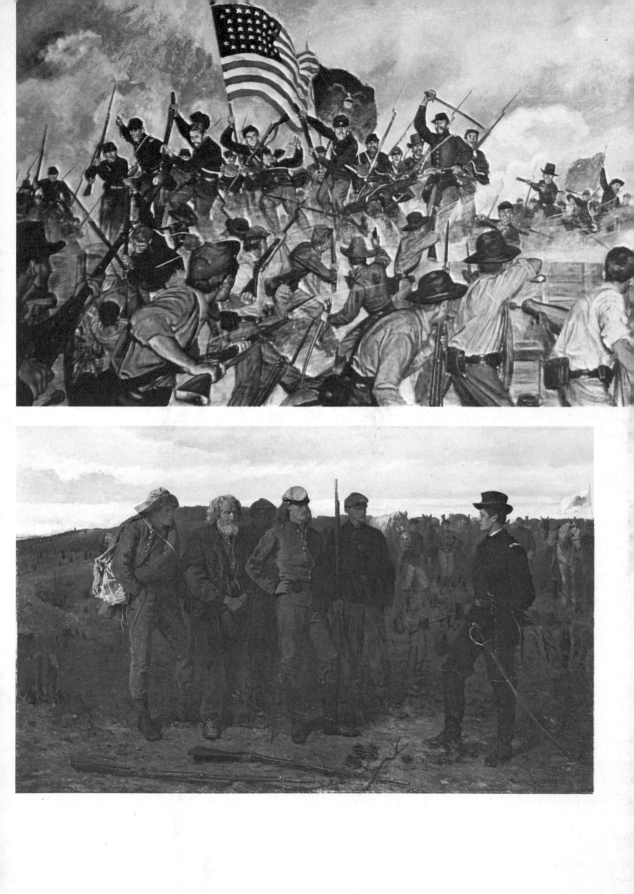

much to the general surprise, accepted the invitation and was then asked to 'set apart formally these grounds to their sacred use by a few appropriate remarks' – an ironical prelude to one of the most illustrious speeches in world history. There was some anxiety as the Presidential party started from the White House about catching the train. The President told the story of the man in Illinois who was being conveyed to the gallows. As the spectators were hurrying past his cart, he called out: 'Boys! you needn't be in such a hurry. There won't be any fun until I get there!'

When they reached Gettysburg, Lincoln, dressed in black and wearing his tall hat and white gauntlets, rode in the middle of a procession through the streets. Edward Everett delivered his immense set-piece oration lasting for about two hours. A hymn was sung and the President of the United States was called on. He appeared, we are told, uneasy. While Everett was speaking, he adjusted his spectacles and read through his manuscript once again. He had made at least six copies of the address. The final draft written in ink covered two pages and was without erasure. When his turn came, he, according to one account, held his pages firmly in both hands. In a well-known painting one of his hands is grasping his lapel. One authority tells us that his voice was thin and high. An Associated Press reporter on the platform noted, however, that 'His marvellous voice careening in fullness of utterance and clearness of tone was perfectly audible on the outskirts of the crowd.'.The same reporter tells us that his words were frequently interrupted by applause. Others present did not recollect it. In fact there was very little time for applause. He spoke for less than three minutes and delivered just under three hundred words. The audience were frankly disappointed. Lincoln himself thought that the speech did not 'scour' and was a flat failure. He said later, 'That speech fell on the audience like a wet blanket. I am distressed about it. I ought to have prepared it with more-care.' Yet, as we have seen, he had made six drafts 'of his few appropriate remarks'. Seward turned to Everett and asked him what he thought of it. Everett replied: 'It is not what I expected from him. I am disappointed. What do you think of it Mr Seward?' Seward replied: 'He has made a failure and I am sorry for it.'

The President was in low spirits on the journey back to Washington. He lay down in the carriage with a wet towel across his forehead. Next day he was not at all well, but got out of bed to see a woman whose husband had been sentenced to be shot. Lincoln wired Meade, asking him to suspend execution. It turned

OPPOSITE A commemorative painting showing Lincoln making his famous Gettysburg address. (Bettmann Archive)

out that he was suffering from smallpox, but still the office-seekers pestered him. 'Come in,' he called from his bed, 'I have something now that I can give to everybody.'

The Press paid little attention to his remarks at Gettysburg. Those who referred to them were inclined to be savage. One paper wrote: 'We pass over the silly remarks of the President. For the credit of the nation we are willing that the veil of oblivion should be dropped over them and that they shall no more be repeated, nor thought of.' The London *Times* wrote, incredibly as it must now seem: 'The ceremony was rendered ludicrous by some of the sallies of that poor President Lincoln who seems determined to play, in this great American union, the part of the famous Governor of Barataria. Anything more dull and commonplace it wouldn't be easy to produce.' But the *Chicago Tribune* saved the honour of the Press with the comment: 'The dedicatory remarks by President Lincoln will live among the annals of man.' The *Springfield Republican* advised its readers: 'Turn back and read it over; it will repay study as a model speech. Strong feeling and a large brain were its parents – a little painstaking its accoucheur.'

The famous words that he delivered are almost too familiar, but can hardly be repeated too often:

Four score and seven years ago our fathers brought forth upon this continent a new nation conceived in liberty and dedicated to the proposition that 'all men are created equal'. Now we are engaged in a great civil war, testing whether that nation, or any nation so conceived and so dedicated, can long endure. We are met on a great battlefield of that war. We have come to dedicate a portion of it as a final resting-place for those who here gave their lives that that nation might live....

Lincoln went on to proclaim:

In a larger sense we cannot dedicate – we cannot consecrate – we cannot hallow this ground. The brave men, living and dead who struggled here have consecrated it far above our poor power to add or detract. The world will little note, nor long remember what we say here, but it can never forget what they did here. It is for us, the living, rather to be dedicated here to the unfinished work which they have thus far so nobly advanced.

Then came the last prolonged overwhelming sentence:

It is rather for us to be here dedicated to the great task remaining before us – that from these honoured dead we take increased devotion to that cause for which they here gave the last full measure of devotion – that we here highly resolve that these dead shall not have died in vain; that this nation, under God, shall have a new birth of freedom; and that government of the people, by the people, for the people, shall not perish from the earth.

The Conscription Act had become law on 3 March 1863. Opposition to it and to drastic actions of Lincoln of doubtful constitutionality formed the basis of Democratic opposition which made some headway in the first half of 1863. The Republicans, appealing to loyal Democrats to join them, campaigned as the National Union Party. Lincoln was unable to attend their major rally on 3 September, but wrote a famous letter to his old friend James C. Conkling, chairman of the committee. 'The signs look better', he declared, but peace could be attained in any one of three ways: first by suppressing the rebellion, which he was earnestly trying to do; second, by giving up the Union, which he would never do; and third, through some sort of compromise, which he believed impossible except on terms of Southern independence. If the South should offer any peace proposals contemplating the maintenance of the Union, Lincoln would neither reject them nor keep them secret.

The election results at the end of 1863 were highly favourable. When Congress assembled in December, Lincoln offered a general plan of reconciliation to the South. He guaranteed full pardon to persons implicated in the rebellion (except a few major offenders), who would take an oath of loyalty to the Constitution and swear to support the emancipation proclamation. In any rebellious state a tenth of the voters could re-establish a democratic government, be recognized as the true government of the state and receive Federal protection. Everyone seemed pleased with his plan, the radical Republicans and the Democrats alike. The year closed on what has been called 'a note of hopefulness and harmony'.

7
Victory
When It
Came
1864-5

I T IS EASY TO THINK OF THE WAR IN 1864 as all over bar the shouting. Churchill, as we have seen, expresses this view. 'It might seem incredible', he writes, 'when we survey the consequences of 1863, that the torments of war should have been prolonged through the whole of 1864 and far into 1865.' But to write in that way seriously underestimates the burden that still lay heavy on the North. Lincoln was still faced with the double Herculean task of winning not only the war but the peace. He was implacable in demanding unconditional surrender and the complete restoration of the Union, but just as inflexible in aiming unswervingly at a real union of hearts, a loyalty – to adapt a phrase of Roger Casement's – that was based on love and not on restraint.

Winning the war itself involved at every point a double endeavour – the military and the political. His opponents could not be defeated unless his own side could be held together, which at one moment seemed almost impossible. And then again, on the political plane he was fighting on two fronts. The leading Republicans thought that he was far too soft in regard to the abolition of slavery and towards the South generally. The Democrats, who at one moment seemed to have an excellent chance of winning the 1864 election, considered that he was much too hard. And the horrifying losses which arose from Grant's methods of military attrition greatly strengthened those who would settle for a negotiated peace.

Crucial dates to keep in mind are 8 March, when Grant came to Washington to be made a Lieutenant-General, and given command of all the forces of the United States; 7 June, when Lincoln was re-selected as Republican candidate for the coming election; and 8 November, when he was re-elected President. It seems best to recite first the military events during the first half of the year, never forgetting the intense political pressures.

Grant arrived by chance during a White House reception. An observer noted that 'he does not march nor quite walk but pitches along as if the next step would bring him on his nose'. He was given a vociferous welcome but made his way as quickly as possible to Lincoln. We are given a picture of the 'lanky and dark-visaged President, slumping as usual in his chair, encumbered by his uncommonly long legs; the short hard-knit general sitting stiffly, ill at ease'. Next day, in the presence of the Cabinet, Lincoln solemnly bestowed on Grant his far-reaching mandate: 'As the country herein entrusts you, so under God it will sustain you . . . with what I here speak for the nation goes my own hearty personal

PREVIOUS PAGES Lee surrenders to Grant on 9 April 1865 at Appomattox Court House. (US National Park Service)

ABOVE General Ulysses S. Grant (second to left, seated) and his staff. On 9 March 1864, Lincoln made Grant a Lieutenant-General, an office which had previously been held by only two Americans – George Washington and Winfield Scott – and placed him in command of all the US forces. (National Archives)

concurrence.' Grant, still visibly uncomfortable, deciphered with difficulty his scribbled notes. 'Mr President,' he said, 'I accept this commission with gratitude for the high honour conferred. . . . I feel the full weight of the responsibilities now devolving on me and know that if they are met it will be due to the armies and above all to the favour of that Providence which leads both nations and men.'

Grant's own account of what Lincoln said to him of his conception of his military role is of deep interest:

In my first interview with Lincoln alone, he stated to me that he had never professed to be a military man or to know how campaigns should be conducted, and never wanted to interfere in them, but that procrastination on the part of commanders and the pressure from the people of the North and Congress, which was always with him, forced him into issuing his 'Military Orders', one, two, three, etc. He did not know but they were all wrong, and did know that some of them were.

Indeed Lincoln went further still. '"All", he said, "he wanted or had ever wanted was someone who would take responsibility and act, and call him for all the assistance he needed, pledging himself to use all the power of the Government in rendering such assistance. . . ." The President told me he did not want to know what I proposed to do.'

Certainly Lincoln struck up a close partnership with Grant as with no previous commander. Field-Marshal Lord Wolseley has written in consequence: 'In the first three years of the Secession War, when Mr Lincoln and Mr Stanton practically controlled the movements of the Federal forces, the Confederates were generally successful. . . . The Northern prospects did not begin to brighten until Mr Lincoln, in March '64, with that unselfish intelligence which distinguished him, abdicated his military functions in favour of General Grant.' This language is disputed by various authorities, who consider the reference to Lincoln's abdication much exaggerated. General Sir Frederick Maurice, in his *Statesmen and Soldiers*, portrays the relationship between Lincoln and Grant as well-nigh perfect and a model partnership between a political and a military chieftain. He supplies many examples of the moral support provided to Grant by Lincoln when things were not going too well.

Churchill is much more critical. He admits that at last on the Northern side there was unity of command and a general capable of exercising it. But he described Grant's overall plan of attrition relying on superior numbers to wear out his opponents as 'brutal

180

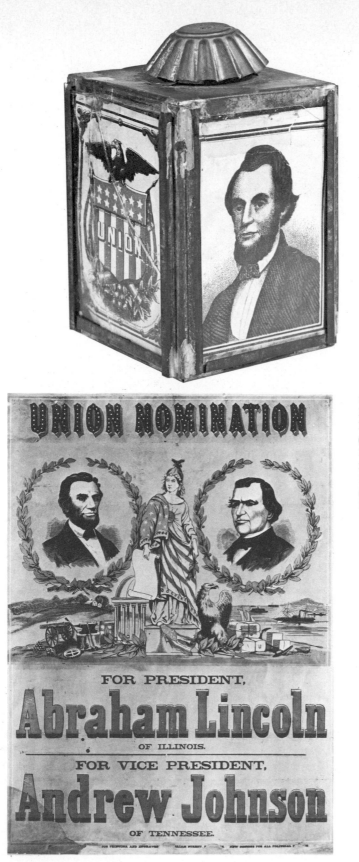

LEFT Lincoln campaign
lantern for the 1864
Presidential election.
(Courtesy of the New-York
Historical Society)
BELOW Poster for the
1864 election.
(Courtesy of the New-York
Historical Society)

and simple'. We can give Lincoln a share of credit for the strategy if we think that credit should be bestowed. Put crudely, its purpose was to bring pressure to bear on the Confederates by a concerted drive from all angles. The obliteration of Lee's army was its primary purpose.

On 4 May the Army of the Potomac crossed the Rapidan. Grant had 122,000 troops to Lee's sixty-two thousand. In that month Grant suffered terrible losses. Churchill reckons that the army of northern Virginia inflicted upon him in thirty days a loss equal to its own total strength. Grant now attempted to make his way into Richmond by the back door, as McClellan had tried to do, and using sea-power, installed his army on the south side of the James River. But he failed to turn Lee's flank and by the end of June resigned himself to trench warfare which lasted till April 1865, when the war was virtually over. 'These performances', says

182

Churchill, 'must be regarded as the negation of generalship.' He adds, admittedly, that they eventually gained their purpose and were a 'deadly form of war'. Even this compliment seems open to question, if we take the Eastern strategy and tactics on their own.

Lincoln's prestige with the general public was enormous, but the politicians were far less friendly. The radicals were described by a close observer as reluctantly admitting that Lincoln's re-election was inevitable. 'The masses are taken in by Lincoln's *apparent* simplicity and good-naturedness, by his awkwardness, by his vulgar jokes, and in the people's belief, that the greater shifter is earnest and honest.' Chase, the Secretary for the Treasury, was aiming hard at the Presidency. Lincoln kept himself well abreast of his intrigues. 'I suppose', he told his secretary, Chase would, 'like the blue-bottle fly, lay his eggs in every rotten

City Point, Virginia, the Union supply base and General Grant's headquarters during the 1864-5 campaign against Petersburg; painting by E. L. Henry. (Addison Gallery of American Art, Phillips Academy, Andover)

spot he can find.' 'But', he continued with his usual tolerance, 'Mr Chase makes a good secretary, and I shall keep him where he is. If he becomes President, all right. I hope we shall never have a worse man. . . . I am entirely indifferent as to his success or failure in these schemes, so long as he does his duty at the head of the Treasury Department.'

But as the casualty lists swelled continuously, the anti-Lincoln radicals gathered confidence. Lincoln supported Grant unfalteringly. A few days after the unsuccessful and costly attack at Cold Harbor, he told Grant: 'I have just read your despatch. I begin to see it. You will succeed. God bless you all.' On a later occasion, undeterred by political anxieties, he wrote to him: 'I have seen your despatch expressing your unwillingness to break your hold where you are. Neither am I willing. Hold on with a bull-dog grip and chew and choke as much as possible.' But large numbers of the public did not feel that way. An attempt was made to sabotage Lincoln's renomination before the Republican Convention at Baltimore. When it came to the point, he was renominated without opposition early in June.

He himself kept fairly clear of the Convention, except to suggest an amendment to the constitution which would bring slavery to an end throughout the United States. The radicals were naturally pleased and even the border states were reconciled. All along, he had been determined to finish the task begun, but when he was re-elected he took it coolly. He told a delegation 'that the Convention had simply concluded it is not best to swop horses while crossing the river and have further concluded that I am not so poor a horse that they might not make a botch of it trying to swop'.

Soon afterwards, he took advantage of a dispute with Chase on a matter of appointments to get rid of him from the Cabinet. The latter asked for a private interview. Lincoln's reply was in his best vein: 'Your resignation of the office of Secretary of the Treasury sent me yesterday is accepted. Of all I have said in commendation of your ability and fidelity, I have nothing to unsay. And yet you and I have reached a point of mutual embarrassment in our official relation which it seems cannot be overcome or longer sustained consistently with the public service.'

But he was far from being out of the wood. To quote Noah Brooks, 'Within a month of the happy and jubilant time following the Convention, everything was once more in confusion in Washington, and the political skies were again darkened by clouds returning after rain.' On 2 July, the last day of the session,

OPPOSITE ABOVE *The Peace Makers*; (from left to right) Generals Sherman and Grant in consultation with Lincoln and Admiral Porter on board the *River Queen*, when Lincoln visited the Union supply base at City Point, Virginia, in March 1865. Painting by C. P. A. Healy. (The White House Collection) OPPOSITE BELOW *Furling the Flags*; painting by R. Brooke. (West Point Museum Collection, US Military Academy)

the radicals in his own party passed a Bill through Congress which nullified his plan for an amnesty and general reconciliation. Lincoln let it lie on the table, on the grounds that he needed to study it, which killed it for the time being. Thereupon, two of the radicals issued a manifesto denouncing him up hill and down dale.

July and August were remembered by those close to Lincoln as the gloomiest months of the entire war. Grant was bogged down in the East, as was Sherman in front of Atlanta. Sherman had learned the hard way at Bull Run and Shiloh, but he was to emerge in the West as second only to Grant in potency. Taking the Civil War as a whole, it is a moot point whether he or Grant proved himself the greater general. At one moment, Washington was threatened by a massive raid of seventeen thousand men under the Confederate General Early. There seemed no clear prospect of peace or victory. A move was made to force Lincoln to withdraw his candidature. Some of his devoted supporters thought he had little chance. A loyal party worker in New York wrote to the Secretary of the Navy representing the views of many: 'There are no Lincoln men. . . . We know not which way to turn.'

On 23 August Lincoln took a curious step. He drafted a letter and asked his colleagues in the Cabinet to sign it on the reverse side without their knowing what was in it. 'This morning,' it ran, 'as for some days past, it seems exceedingly probable that this Administration will not be re-elected. When it will be my duty to so co-operate with the President elect, as to save the Union between the election and the inauguration; as he will have secured his election on such ground that he cannot possibly save it afterwards.' Whatever the result of the election, Lincoln was determined that the war should be won. After his re-election, he explained the unusual, rather moving letter:

You will remember that this was written at a time six days before the Democratic Chicago nomination convention, when as yet we had no adversary, and seemed to have no friends. I then solemnly resolved on the course of action indicated above. I resolved, in case of the election of General McClellan, being certain that he would be the candidate, that I would see him and talk matters over with him, I would say: 'General, the election has demonstrated that you are stronger, have more influence with the American people than I. Now let us together – you with your influence and I with all the executive power of the Government – try to save the country. You raise as many troops as you possibly can for this final trial, and I will devote all my energy to assisting and finishing the War.'

186

The audacity, indeed the eccentricity, not to mention the humility of this idea, was pure Lincoln.

The Democratic Convention duly met in Chicago on 29 August. A resolution was passed which was widely summarized as announcing 'the war is a failure'. The constitution was held as 'disregarded in every part'. Justice, humanity, liberty and the public welfare demanded that 'immediate efforts be made for the cessation of hostilities, with a view to an ultimate convention of

Cartoon by Thomas Nash, which appeared in *Harper's Weekly* during Lincoln's re-election campaign of 1864, depicting the growing threat of a North–South compromise. (John Frost Historical Newspaper Collection)

the states, or other peaceable means to the end that, at the earliest practicable moment, peace may be restored on the basis of the Federal Union of the states'. This came close to a policy of peace at any price, though the Presidential candidate, our old friend McClellan in a new capacity, repudiated that implication. If we wish to say that the resolution was based on fantasy, we must at the same time remind ourselves that only a week before, Lincoln was privately admitting that he had little chance of winning.

Suddenly overnight the whole atmosphere changed. Sherman telegraphed: 'Atlanta is ours and fairly won.' The North exploded in delight. Lincoln called for a day of thanksgiving 'for the signal successes vouchsafed by Providence' at Atlanta and at Mobile (captured by Admiral Farragut). Directed by Lincoln and Grant, the dashing young Federal General Sheridan brought over-whelming force to bear in the Shenandoah Valley. By the middle of October he had cleared it and gone far to ravish it. 'Little remained in the valley to sustain man or beast.' The back door into the Northern territory was finally closed. Now there was a rush even among the most hostile radicals to climb on the Lincoln band-wagon. Lincoln, however, was leaving nothing to chance. When he decided to fight, he decided to win. Agar lays emphasis on fraudulent methods adopted, it must be assumed with Lincoln's knowledge. The great majority of the public were, however, with him. The result, when it came, was clear cut, though Churchill calls it a 'narrow victory'.

Lincoln received 2,203,831 ballots to McClellan's 1,797,019, a majority of more than 400,000, with Lincoln carrying every state except Kentucky, Delaware and New Jersey (the rebel states were of course excluded). His majority in the Electoral College would be 212 to twenty-one. The soldiers were given the chance to come home to vote and went strongly for Lincoln. His secretary, Hay, recalls some of his remarks while waiting for the verdict: 'It is singular', he observed, 'that I, who am not a vindictive man should always, except once, have been before the people in canvasses marked by great bitterness. When I came to Congress it was a quiet time, but always, except that, the contests in which I have been prominent have been marked with great rancour.' The first returns began to look favourable. Lincoln sent them over to Mrs Lincoln. 'She is more anxious than I,' he commented. Someone expressed pleasure that one of his radical opponents had been defeated. 'You have more of that feeling of personal resentment than I,' said Lincoln. 'Perhaps I have too little of it, but I never thought it paid. A man has no time to spend half his life in quarrels. If any man ceases to attack me, I never remember the past against him.' During the evening he recalled a strange dream that came to him after the election of 1860. He saw himself in a huge mirror; his face had two distinct images, one nearly superimposed on the other, one face looked paler than the other. The dream had troubled him and Mrs Lincoln had taken it for a sign. Her husband would be elected for a second period, but the pale face signified that he would not live through it.

The next night, a crowd marched to the White House and serenaded Lincoln triumphantly. 'The election', he told them, 'along with its incidental and undesirable strife has done us good too. It has demonstrated that a people's government can sustain a national election in the midst of a great civil war. Until now it has not been known to the world that this was a possibility.'

The last stages of the war were now being entered. The gallant defenders were being steadily overwhelmed. On 12 November Sherman, persuading Lincoln and Grant with some little difficulty, set off 'to march through Georgia to the shores of the Atlantic'. His army lived on the country, destroying all farms, villages, towns, railroads and public works within his reach. 'He left behind him a blackened trail and hatreds which pursue his memory to this day. "War is Hell" and he certainly made it so' (Churchill). He reached Savannah on the ocean coast in time to send the news of its fall as a Christmas present to Lincoln. Meanwhile, the Federal General Thomas routed the Confederates on 15 December, in the battle of Nashville. At last the net was beginning to close.

Lincoln hated war, but he saw little hope of peace negotiations until the South surrendered. In his annual message in December 1864 he said of Jefferson Davis 'He would accept nothing short of severance of the Union, precisely what we will not and cannot give. . . . He does not attempt to deceive us; he affords us no excuse to deceive ourselves.' The elder statesman Francis Blair obtained permission from Lincoln to visit Davis and brought back a promise that if Lincoln would receive peace commissioners, Davis would appoint such emissaries at once, with a view to bringing peace to the two countries. Lincoln was not going to be caught that way. He was ready to receive any agent 'whom he [Davis], or any other influential person now resisting the national authority, may informally send me with the view of securing peace to the people of our one common country'. He made it abundantly plain that

Sherman's 'March to the Sea'. On 16 November Sherman set out with his army from Atlanta to march across two hundred and fifty miles of enemy territory to the Atlantic. (Library of Congress)

peace was impossible until the South laid down their arms and submitted to the national authority.

Eventually, on 3 February, Lincoln and Seward sat down with three Confederate representatives in the cabin of a naval vessel which lay off Fortress Monroe. The diminutive Alexander Stephens, whom Lincoln had always esteemed since their days in Congress, was one of the delegates. He arrived bundled in a tremendous overcoat, with numerous scarves and vestments.

The President remarked afterwards that it was 'the smallest nubbin for so much shucking that he had ever seen'. They argued away for several hours, inevitably without progress. One of the delegates reminded Lincoln that Charles I had negotiated with persons in arms against his government. Lincoln replied that he was not 'posted' on history. All that he distinctly remembered about the matter was that Charles had lost his head. Hunter, a Confederate delegate, said that he understood that Lincoln regarded the leaders of the Confederacy as traitors. Lincoln granted; 'That was about the size of it.' After a moment's silence Hunter smiled: 'Well, Mr Lincoln,' he said, 'we have about concluded that we shall not be hanged as long as you are President – if we behave ourselves.' The conference predictably came to nothing.

Lincoln had let it be known during the talks that he still favoured compensation to owners of emancipated slaves. When, however, he read a proposal to his Cabinet to appropriate $400 million in reimbursement to slave-owners, provided that fighting stopped by 1 April, they would not hear of it. They rejected the idea unanimously. 'You are all opposed to me', he said regretfully, and being not only the most magnanimous of men but an astute politician, requested that nothing should be said about the proposal outside the Cabinet.

Sherman's troops destroying railroads during their 'March to the Sea' in the winter of 1864-5. 'We are not only fighting hostile armies, but a hostile people, and we must make old and young, rich and poor, feel the hand of war, as well as their organized armies.' (Library of Congress)

He was beaten there but, as far as humanly possible, he kept the ultimate decisions in his own hands. Lee tried to start some military negotiations with Grant, who asked Lincoln for instructions through Stanton. Lincoln at once drafted a reply for Stanton to send him:

The President directs me to say to you that he wishes you to have no conference with General Lee unless it be for the capitulation of Gen. Lee's army, or on some minor and purely military matter. He instructs me to say that you are not to decide, discuss, or confer upon any political question. Such questions the President holds in his own hands; and will submit them to no military conferences or conventions. Meantime you are to press to the utmost your military advantages.

On 31 January, the amendment to the Constitution abolishing slavery throughout the length and breadth of the Republic had been finally carried. 'There was an explosion,' said Noah Brooks, 'a storm of cheers, the like of which probably no Congress of the United States ever heard before.' 'Strong men embraced each other with tears.'

And so to the second inaugural, to be ranked as the greatest of all Lincoln's speeches along with the Gettysburg address – in language its equal, in its generosity of spirit still more profound. The inaugural procession made its way through the mud, with a cold, gusty wind blowing. After taking the oath in the Senate Chamber, the official party emerged on the portico before the vast crowd which, we are told, 'extended as far as the eye could reach and broke in waves along the outer edges of the Capitol, among the budding foliage of the grounds beyond'. They greeted the President with tremendous applause. Lincoln had had one or two preoccupations, in addition to the historic responsibility of the moment. The Vice-President, Johnson, was recovering from typhoid fever, had taken an unaccustomed tumbler of whisky and made an unhappy showing inside the Senate Chamber. 'Johnson is either drunk or crazy', whispered Gideon Welles into Stanton's ear. Lincoln had lowered his head, looking down, we are told, 'in deep humiliation'. Always prompt to act in an emergency, he was heard to tell an official: 'Do not let Johnson speak outside.' But now he was absorbed in a nobler theme.

Every word was clear and audible as the ringing if somewhat shrill tones of Lincoln's voice sounded over the vast concourse. 'Fellow-countrymen,' he began, 'at this second appearing to take the oath, there is less occasion for an extended address than there was at the first.' He trusted that the progress 'of our arms' was reasonably satisfactory and encouraging to all. He held high hopes for the future, but ventured no prediction concerning it. Then came the incomparable sentences:

Neither party expected for the war, the magnitude, or the duration, which it has already attained. Neither anticipated that the *cause* of the conflict might cease with, or even before, the conflict itself should cease. Each looked for an easier triumph, and a result less fundamental and astounding. Both read the same Bible, and pray to the same God; and each invokes His aid against the other. . . . The prayers of both could not be answered; that of neither has been answered fully. . . .

No one on the point of total victory could surpass that for magnanimity. In the words that followed, he was careful to lay blame, in so far as he laid it, on North and South alike:

If we shall suppose that American Slavery is one of those offences which, in the providence of God, must needs come, but which having continued through His appointed time, He now wills to remove, and that He gives to both North and South, this terrible war, as the woe due to those by whom the offence came, shall we discern therein any departure from those divine attributes which the believers in a Living God always ascribe to Him?

He seemed determined to dwell on his conviction, now more than ever emergent, that the ways of the Almighty were just:

Yet if God wills that it continue, until all the wealth piled by the bondman's two hundred and fifty years of unrequited toil shall be sunk, and until every drop of blood drawn with the lash, shall be paid by another drawn with the sword, as was said three thousand years ago, so still it must be said 'The judgements of the Lord are true and righteous altogether.'

Finally, the most characteristic phrases of all:

With malice toward none; with charity for all; with firmness in the right, as God gives us to see the right, let us strive on to finish the work we are in; to bind up the nation's wounds; to care for him who shall have borne the battle, and for his widow and his orphan – to do all which may achieve and cherish a just and lasting peace, among ourselves and with all nations.

There was strong applause at the end, not perhaps an ovation. Lincoln wrote about it soon afterwards: 'I expect it to wear as well as, perhaps better than any I have produced, but I believe it is not immediately popular.'

There was no lack of enthusiasm for him at the inaugural ball that evening. He is said to have shaken hands with more than six thousand persons, and many more could not get near him. Walt

Whitman wrote: 'I saw Mr Lincoln, drest all in black, with white kid gloves and a claw-hammer coat, receiving as in duty bound, shaking hands, looking very disconsolate, and as if he would give anything to be somewhere else.' Frederick Douglass, the Negro leader, was held up by the police at the entrance. Lincoln sent out for him and warmly shook his hand. 'Douglass, I saw you in the crowd to-day, listening to my inaugural address. There is no man's opinion that I value more than yours; what do you think of it?' Douglass told him: 'Mr Lincoln, it was a sacred effort.' And Lincoln smiled: 'I am glad you like it.' Lincoln saw a young officer who had lost a leg and was hobbling on crutches, and moved across to him, taking his hand in his own he said: 'God bless you, my boy.' The lieutenant was overwhelmed. 'Oh! I'd lose another leg for a man like that', he whispered to his companion.

Sherman was now marching northwards and would soon unite with Grant by land. At Grant's invitation, Mr and Mrs Lincoln visited Grant at his headquarters. Tad went with them – 'the complete embodiment of animal spirits', as Noah Brooks called him. 'The irrepressible sprite that brightened the weary years which Lincoln passed in Washington.' He consoled his parents a little for the irreplaceable Willie. Of the endless stories about Tad, one only can be repeated here. Day in, day out the office-seekers haunted the White House. Sometimes, the lines extended all the way down the stairs and nearly to the main entrance. Tad used to interrogate these persons with a mixture of sympathy and artfulness. Once he mounted guard at the foot of the public staircase and levied toll on all who passed up it. He demanded 'five cents for the benefit of the sanitary fund'. The visitors entertained the no doubt false impression that in this way their chances were strengthened.

With Meade, Lincoln surveyed the battlefields at Petersburg – the dead, the wounded and the prisoners, visibly affected as always in the presence of suffering. When an officer told him that he had seen a young Confederate soldier moaning for his mother and then dying, 'Lincoln's eyes filled with tears and his voice was choked as he repeated the familiar phrase: "Robbing the cradle and the grave".' But for all his softness of heart, no one doubted that he had all along been a man of steel. Grant asked him: 'Mr President, did you at any time doubt the final success of the cause?' Lincoln answered emphatically: 'Never for a moment!'

Richmond fell. Lincoln wired to his Secretary of War: 'It is certain now that Richmond is in our hands and I think that I would

Lincoln and his wife greeting guests during a reception at the White House early in 1865. (Lincoln National Life Foundation, Fort Wayne, Ind.)

go there tomorrow.' To Stanton's pleas of caution he replied: 'I will take care of myself.' With an escort of ten seamen, he plodded two miles through the streets of the rebel capital. The general public seemed dazed, but the Negroes paid heartfelt tribute. 'Bless the Lord, here is the great Messiah!' cried out an old Negro, when he recognized Lincoln. 'I knew him as soon as I saw him. He's been in my heart for long years. Glory, hallelujah!' With this he fell on his knees. But Lincoln told him: 'Don't kneel to me. You must kneel to God only and thank Him for your freedom.' He drove on to Jefferson Davis's former headquarters. When an officer suggested to him that Davis should be hanged, Lincoln replied gently: 'Judge not, that ye be not judged.' When the General in charge asked him about the treatment of the conquered people in Richmond, he replied: 'If I were in your place I'd let them up easy.'

The President hurried back to visit Seward, who had suffered severe injuries in a fall from his carriage. That night, 9 April, a telegram came from Grant: 'General Lee surrendered the army of Northern Virginia this morning on terms proposed by myself.' He set out the terms which were in the spirit of Lincoln's instructions. No surrender scene had ever done quite so much credit to the participants. Lee arrived in resplendent uniform. Grant apologized for being untidily dressed and, showing the utmost sensitivity,

197

seemed reluctant to discuss the matter in hand. Lee had to bring him to the point: 'I suppose, General Grant, that the object of our present meeting is fully understood? I asked to see you to ascertain upon what terms you would receive the surrender of my army.' Grant mentioned the terms already communicated: 'Officers and men surrendered to be paroled and disqualified from taking up arms again until properly exchanged, and all arms, ammunition and supplies to be delivered up as captured property.' Grant asked Lee whether he had any request. Yes, he had; that the men should be allowed to keep their own horses as they would be badly needed for the spring ploughing. Grant agreed, and Lee expressed his gratitude: 'This will have the best possible effect upon the men. It will be very gratifying and will do much towards conciliating our people.' Grant made a simple announcement: 'The war is over; the rebels are our countrymen again and the best sign of rejoicing after the victory will be to abstain from all demonstrations in the field.' Lincoln himself could not have spoken better.

Lincoln, victorious at last, spoke to an immense crowd from the White House lawn. He exhibited no trace of triumph. His mind was concerned only with laying the foundations of a lasting peace. He was no Shakespearean scholar, but he knew some of the plays well. *Macbeth* was his favourite. On the way back to Washington, his mind had dwelt on the lines:

> Duncan is in his grave;
> After life's fitful fever he sleeps well;
> Treason has done his worst; nor steel, nor poison,
> Malice domestic, foreign levy, nothing
> Can touch him further.

There was much talk of confiscation and mass disfranchisement of Southern citizens. Lincoln appealed for forgiveness before all else. He spoke almost pedantically. 'We all agree', he said, 'that the seceded States are out of their proper practical relation with the Union, . . . let us all join in doing the acts necessary in restoring the proper practical relations between these States and the Union, and each forever after, innocently indulge his own opinion whether, in doing the acts, he brought the States from without into the Union, or only gave them proper assistance, they never having been out of it.' The thought and feeling were ingenious and imaginative, but the words would be difficult for a large crowd to follow, and their enthusiasm waned.

14 April was Good Friday. Grant and the Cabinet waited for

ABOVE The fall of Richmond on the
night of 2 April 1865. As thousands
fled from the city, the garrison set
fire to factories, arsenals and
warehouses to make sure that
nothing of value fell into Union
hands. By the following morning,
most of the centre of the city had
been destroyed. (The Museum of the
Confederacy, Richmond)

OVERLEAF The burnt-out
ruins of Richmond after the
fall of the city in April 1865.
(Library of Congress)

Lincoln at his office, where he returned from the War Department. Lincoln had had another dream, one that had come to him several times before an important event, usually a Union victory – the vision of a phantom ship moving very rapidly towards a dark, indefinite shore. 'It must', he thought, 'foretell the expected news from Sherman that the last Confederate forces opposite him had also capitulated.' Lincoln spoke kindly to the Cabinet of Lee and other officers and of all the brave men who had fought in the Confederate army. He was glad that Congress was not in session. He hoped to have established friendly relations with the Southern states before it met. 'There are many in Congress,' he said, 'who possess feelings of hate and vindictiveness in which I do not sympathize and cannot participate.' He hoped there would be no persecutions, no bloody work; enough blood had been shed. He would join in no vengeful actions, even towards the worst of the secessionists. 'Frighten them out of the country,' he said, 'open the gates, let down the bars, scare them off' – he waved his hands as though shooing sheep out of a loft.

He and Mary went for a drive together in the afternoon. They talked about the life ahead of them. 'We must both be cheerful in the future,' said Lincoln. 'Between the war and the loss of our darling Willie we have both been very miserable.' But sadness was not his dominating mood. 'The Friday', wrote Mary Lincoln later, 'I never saw him so supremely cheerful. His manner was even playful. During the drive he was so gay that I said to him laughingly "Dear husband, you almost startle me by your great cheerfulness," and he replied, "Well I may feel so, Mary. I consider this day the war has come to a close." ' It was in that connection that he said that they must both be more cheerful in future.

At half past eight, the White House coachman brought the President, Mrs Lincoln and two guests to Ford's Theatre to see a play called *Our American Cousin*. Cheers echoed and re-echoed as an usher conducted the party to a flag-draped box. Their guests, Major Rathbone and Miss Harris, sat towards the front. Mrs Lincoln sat farther back and the President lay back wearily in a hair-cloth rocking-chair near the rear of the box. The White House guard who had been assigned to protect the President went out apparently for a drink. The third act was in progress. Lincoln was thoroughly enjoying it. Major Rathbone took Miss Harris's hand in his. Not to be outdone, the President took Mrs Lincoln's. 'What will Miss Harris think of me hanging on to you so?' she asked, obviously pleased. 'She won't think anything of it', replied

OPPOSITE Lincoln photographed with his youngest son Tad on 10 April 1865. (Radio Times Hulton Picture Library)

203

the President affectionately. She drew closer to him for a brief moment.

A dark-haired man strolled down the aisle of the Dress Circle and slipped into the President's box, passing first through the outer door which he made fast and then the inner door. The man was John Wilkes Booth, an unbalanced young actor who had won considerable celebrity through his personal glamour and, incidentally, by his athleticism on the stage. He loved the South with a romantic passion and yearned to perform some heroic deed that might atone for her defeat and his own failure to take up arms on her behalf. A strange personal class-feeling towards Lincoln added fuel to his flame: 'That Sectional Candidate should never have been President, the votes were *doubled* to seat him, he was smuggled through Maryland to the White House. . . . This man's appearance, his pedigree, his coarse low jokes and anecdotes, his vulgar similes and his frivolity, are a disgrace to the seat he holds. . . .' Booth's father had been the most famous tragedian in America, but suffered from time to time from fits of insanity. The son had inherited some part of this disposition and a somewhat smaller part of the histrionic genius. Years before, a fortune-teller had made this forecast:

Ah, you've a bad hand; the lines all cris-cras. It's full enough of sorrow – full of trouble – trouble in plenty, everywhere I look. You'll break hearts, they'll be nothing to you. You'll die young, and leave many to mourn you, many to love you too, but you'll be rich, generous and free with your money. You're born under an unlucky star. You've got in your hand a thundering crowd of enemies – not one friend – you'll make a bad end, and have plenty to love you afterwards. You'll have a fast life, short – but a grand one. Now, young sir, I've never seen a worse hand, and I wish I hadn't seen it, but every word I've told you is true by the signs. You'd best turn a missionary or a priest and try to escape it.

He knew the theatre well and also the play. He chose a moment when attention would be centred on the stage and when the stage itself would be almost empty. In his right hand he carried a small Derringer pistol, in his left a dagger. He pulled the trigger and shot Lincoln through the back of the head, mortally wounding him. He shouted dramatically: *'Sic semper tyrannus!'* words used by Brutus when he killed Caesar, and, moreover, the motto of Virginia. Major Rathbone threw himself at Booth but Booth stabbed him and jumped over the box railing to the stage eleven feet below. The spur of his riding-boot caught in the flag which draped the box damaging his leg. Limping though he was, he made an

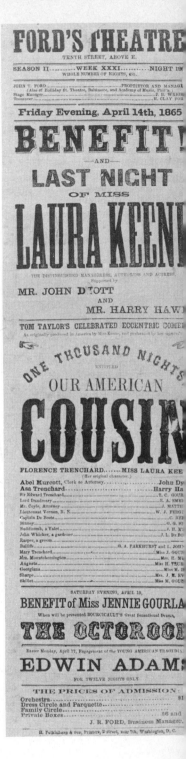

After Lincoln was shot, he was carried to a house across the street from Ford's Theatre. He died the following morning at 7.22 without gaining consciousness. Drawing by Herman Faber. (Library of Congress)

astonishing escape, though later he was hunted down and shot.

Mary Lincoln gave a piercing scream. Panic and pandemonium prevailed. Someone shouted 'He has shot the President!' A young Army surgeon climbed into the box. 'Oh Doctor, is he dead?', cried Mary Lincoln. 'Will you take charge of him? Do what you can for him. Oh my dear husband, my dear husband!' The doctor could see at a glance that the President's injury was fatal, but all night the struggle for his life continued. He was taken to a small house near the theatre and placed in a room on the ground floor. Mary Lincoln spent the night in the parlour opposite. Army officers, doctors and members of the Government gathered rapidly. Every now and then Mary was allowed to see the President. 'Live,' she cried, as she bent over him, 'you must live!' Then she added, 'Bring Tad, he will speak to Tad. He loves him so.' And, back in the parlour, she said, talking to herself: 'Why did he not shoot me instead of my husband? I have tried to be so careful of him, fearing something would happen and his life seemed to be more precious now than ever.' A little later, she cried out: 'I must go to him.' About 7 a.m. she was brought in to see him for the last time. Seeing him as he was by that time, and hearing his groans, she fell into a faint and was gently removed. Robert, who had stood beside the bed for many hours, went with her.

There had never been any chance of Lincoln surviving, though the unconscious will to live was astounding. At 7.22 it was all over. Stanton, the Secretary of State for War, had spoken contemptuously of Lincoln in the past, but in the last three years, had worked with him in an ever more fruitful partnership. He found immediate words which were not unworthy: 'Now he belongs to the ages.'

There had never been a demonstration of grief in America like that which followed. His coffin was eventually conveyed to Springfield along the route which he had followed when he moved upwards to the White House. But much was to happen first. Carl Sandburg in his last volume sums up memorably:

THERE was a funeral.
It took long to pass its many given points.
Many millions of people saw it and personally moved in it and were part of its procession.
The line of march ran seventeen hundred miles.
As a dead march nothing like it had ever been attempted before.
Like the beginning and the end of the Lincoln Administration, it had no precedents to go by.
It was garish, vulgar, massive, bewildering, chaotic.

208

Lincoln's funeral procession in Lower Pennsylvania Avenue, Washington. It was the start of a 1,700-mile journey which was to take the body back to Springfield, Illinois, for burial. (Courtesy Chicago Historical Society)

Also it was simple, final, majestic, august.

In spite of some of its mawkish excess of show and various maudlin proceedings, it gave solemn unforgettable moments to millions of people who had counted him great, warm and lovable.

Many thousands of sermons were preached in the days following his death and many glowing orations delivered. On the whole, the Press rose to the occasion in articles that are still significant. Perhaps the words of the New York *Herald* were the most representative: 'A new kind of historian', said the *Herald*, would be required 'to comprehend the genius of a character so externally uncouth, so pathetically simple, so unfathomably penetrating, so irresolute and yet so irresistible, so bizarre, grotesque, droll, wise

Andrew Johnson, Lincoln's Vice-President during his second term of office, and President from 1865 to 1869. (Radio Times Hulton Picture Library)

and perfectly beneficent as the great original thinker and statesman for whose death the whole land, even in the midst of victories unparalleled, is today draped in mourning.' General Lee's reaction corresponded with his character. He said that when he dispossessed himself of the command of the rebel forces, he kept in mind President Lincoln's benignity, and surrendered as much to the

210

latter's goodness as to Grant's artillery. He regretted Mr Lincoln's death as much as any man in the North, and believed him to be the epitome of magnanimity and good faith. Jefferson Davis paid tribute later in his own fashion: 'The news of the assassination was to me very sad, for I felt that Mr Johnson [the new President] was a malignant man, and without the power or generosity which I believed Mr Lincoln possessed.'

But other notes were struck, jarring and indeed sinister. A small extremist element from both ends of the spectrum exulted. In front of the New York Post Office a man saluted someone: 'Did you hear of Abe's last joke?' In a few moments, he was being beaten up by a crowd crying: 'Hang him! Kill him! Hang the bastard up!' And the same kind of remark produced the same response everywhere. What was much more disquieting was that many of those who eulogized him vehemently were denying in the same breath the essence of his teaching. A caucus of the Republican Party radicals met to consider 'a line of policy less conciliatory than that of Mr Lincoln'. They were shocked at the murder, but the feeling was general that the accession of Johnson to the Presidency 'would prove a godsend to the country'. Senator Wade greeted the new President: 'Mr Johnson, I thank God that you are here. Lincoln had too much of the milk of human kindness to deal with these damn rebels. Now they will be dealt with according to their deserts.' Many of the sermons expressed the same point of view in theological language.

Today it sounds enlightened, progressive and ethical to hold out the hand of friendship to the South and also to press for immediate extension of full civic rights to the Negro. At the time of Lincoln's death, it seemed highly dubious whether these two immediate aspirations were compatible. The radical abolitionists, the dominant influence on the winning side, were demanding universal suffrage for the black population in the Southern states, although in most of the Northern states it was not yet granted. The motives of the abolitionists were a peculiar mixture of humanitarian feeling and personal vindictiveness.

In the event, Congress was strong enough to set aside the plans Lincoln had foreshadowed, to over-rule and come near to destroying his successor Johnson, and to pass legislation which produced a Negro majority in five states. Governments under military supervision were set up, composed of 'carpet-baggers' (fortune hunters from the North) and 'scallywags' (Southern Quislings). Twelve years after Lincoln's death, the Federal troops left the

South and the 'carpet-baggers' collapsed, leaving small advantage
to the Negroes apart from the overwhelming fact of emancipation,
and far-reaching persistent hatreds among the white population.
Lincoln's prestige was so enormous, his outlook so elevated, his
political skill so unlimited, that he might – one can only say
might – have found the way to provide justice for the Negro along
with mercy to the Southern white population.

Emerson – like many others – refused to endorse the policy of
conciliation and pardon which Lincoln was convinced would
have the sanction of the people and the country. Yet in a curious
contradictory way he saw him as 'a heroic figure in the centre of a
heroic epoch – the true history of the American people in his time'.
Tolstoy would say of him: 'The greatness of Aristotle or Kant is as
insignificant compared with the greatness of Buddha, Moses and
Christ. The greatness of Napoleon, Caesar or Washington is moon-
light by the sun of Lincoln. His example is universal and will last
thousands of years. Washington was a typical American, Napoleon
was a typical Frenchman, but Lincoln was humanitarian as broad
as the world. He was bigger than his country – bigger than all the
Presidents put together.'

The opinion-forming classes of England did not on the whole
come well out of the American Civil War. The working classes did
something to redeem the national honour. Many forms of labour
organization in England and on the Continent sent messages in
one form or another; they could never forget the great American
statesman who had said: 'Working men are the basis of all government.' The London Press, including *The Times*, made rather
feeble amends. *Punch*, which had continuously belittled Lincoln,
emerged however with credit. It published verses by Tom Taylor,
author of *Our American Cousin* which Lincoln had been watching
when he was shot. The sincerity of the apology is patent:

> Beside this corpse, that bears for winding-sheet
>   The Stars and Stripes he lived to rear anew
> Between the mourners at his head and feet
>   Say, scurril-jester, is there room for YOU?
>
> Yes, he had lived to shame me from my sneer,
>   To lame my pencil, and confute my pen –
> To make me own this kind of princes' peer,
>   This rail-splitter a true-born king of men.

Queen Victoria and her husband at least had had no reason to

212

"*THIS IS A WHITE MAN'S GOVERNMENT.*"

apologize. She could and did write to Mrs Lincoln: 'No one can better appreciate than I can, who am myself UTTERLY BROKEN-HEARTED by the loss of my own beloved husband, who was the LIGHT of my life, my stay – MY ALL – what your suffering must be; and I earnestly pray that you may be supported by Him to whom alone the sorely stricken can look for comfort.' Mary Lincoln replied: 'Madam, I have received the letter, which Your Majesty has had the kindness to write, & am deeply grateful for its expressions of tender sympathy, coming as they do, from a heart which from its own sorrows can appreciate the *intense grief* I now endure. Accept, Madam, the assurance of my heartfelt thanks & believe me in the deepest sorrow. Your Majesty's sincere and grateful friend.' Mary Lincoln and Queen Victoria had been born within a few months of each other. They were both still under fifty. Queen Victoria was to live another thirty-six years and leave a noble legacy. Mary Lincoln was to live almost half as long; her life was destroyed with Lincoln's. In a beautiful image at her funeral, Dr Reed likened Mary and Abraham Lincoln to two pine trees growing so close to one another that their branches and roots intertwined. When one tree was struck down by lightning, the other seemed at first unharmed, 'but they had virtually both been killed at the same time. With the one that lingered it was slow death from the same cause.'

OPPOSITE Mary Todd Lincoln, who survived her husband by seventeen years. At her funeral, Dr Reed said of her relationship with Lincoln: '. . . they had virtually both been killed at the same time. With the one that lingered it was slow death from the same cause.' (Radio Times Hulton Picture Library)

8 'As God gives us to see the Right'

'TODAY,' SAYS HERBERT AGAR, 'the world thinks of Lincoln not as the saviour of the United States, but as the great emancipator.' Mr Agar goes on to indicate that in his opinion this is a false perspective. Words written by Lincoln in October 1863 should not be lost sight of: 'We are in a Civil War. In such cases there is always a main question, but in this case that question is a perplexing compound – Union and slavery.'

Lincoln always hated slavery. His consistency in that respect cannot fairly be questioned. There is the well-known story told by his cousin John Hanks of his seeing a slave auction at New Orleans, when barely grown up, and saying fiercely: 'If ever I get a chance to hit that thing, I'll hit it hard.' Whether or not textually accurate, the thirty years that followed bear witness to its essential veracity. Slavery as an institution he denounced on many occasions. In the first of his historic orations at Peoria in 1854, he referred to 'the monstrous injustice of slavery itself'. 'If the Negro is a MAN, why then my ancient faith teaches me that "all men are created equal", and that "there can be no moral right in connection with one man's making a slave of another".' But in this speech, as in so many other later ones, his basic attack was concentrated not on the *existence* of slavery, but on the *extension* of it. In other words, he was not an abolitionist. He did not take a stand for the abolition of slavery at that time, or indeed till near the end of the Civil War, and only then, it can be argued, because his hand was forced by circumstances and pressures. The distinction in Lincoln's thought between the existence and the extension of slavery was fundamental. His refusal to allow the extension of the evil thing while permitting it to continue where it existed already was the essential feature of his election programme in 1860. He might even have seemed a bulwark in the eyes of the Southerners against the Northern abolitionists.

Yet it is a historical fact that his election as President in November 1860 was the signal for South Carolina to secede from the Union, followed by six other states, before his inauguration in March 1861, and by four more soon afterwards. Were they utterly mistaken in their conviction that the triumph of Lincoln sounded the death-knell of slavery sooner or later, and sooner rather than later? Was the distinction between the existence of slavery and the extension of slavery one that could continue indefinitely? 'The real issue in this controversy', declared Lincoln in his last debate with Douglas in 1858, 'is the sentiment on the part of one class that looks upon the institution of slavery *as a*

218

wrong, and of another class that *does not* look upon it as a wrong. The sentiment that contemplates the institution of slavery in this country as wrong, is the sentiment of the Republican Party.' The Southern slave-owners could be forgiven for believing that however humane his intention, this man – Abraham Lincoln – represented the ultimate threat to their system.

It is, nevertheless, as certain as anything can be in history that, if Lincoln had declared for the immediate abolition of slavery before the Civil War, or in its early stages, he would never in fact have achieved that purpose. In other words, the South would 'have got away with' secession, and slavery would have continued thereafter – who knows for how long? In the first place, the four border states would have left the Union which, in itself, would have been decisive and fatal. Quite apart from that, Lincoln would never have been able to hold together what was in the event a war-winning coalition.

But in this matter he could not preserve his initial posture indefinitely in the face of radical 'abolitionist pressures' in his own party and more or less enlightened opinion abroad. In September 1862, he set his hand to a proclamation announcing that on 1 January 1863, all slaves within any state in rebellion should be immediately freed. No doubt in retrospect this was a turning-point nationally and internationally.

But it was far from disposing of the slavery issue, even on paper. It applied, be it noted, only to slaves in the rebellious states. The border slave-owning states remained as great a problem as ever, while the abolitionist pressures on Lincoln mounted remorselessly. Another element in his thought became more and more evident – his determination to win a military victory indeed, but just as emphatically to win the hearts and minds of the South rather than crush them, degrade them or ruin them.

As time went on, the movement for abolition became irresistible. In December, after his re-election as President, Lincoln asked Congress to pass the amendment to the Constitution abolishing slavery throughout the United States. It was passed by Congress in January 1865, though not finally ratified until the end of the year, by which time Lincoln was dead. To the end of his life he was hoping to bring about a social revolution and a reconciliation between North and South at the same time. Who can say that if he had lived, he would not have succeeded?

The contention remains that it was Lincoln's primary purpose throughout the war to save the Union. It is not difficult to quote

219

considered words of Lincoln to that effect. In the famous letter to Horace Greeley of August 1862, Lincoln wrote:

My paramount object in this struggle is to save the Union. . . . If I could save the Union without freeing any slave, I would do it; and if I could save it by freeing all the slaves, I would do it; and if I could save it by freeing some and leaving others alone, I would also do that. What I do about slavery and the coloured race, I do because I believe it helps to save the Union; and what I forbear, I forbear because I do not believe it would help to save the Union. I shall do less whenever I shall believe what I am doing hurts the cause, and I shall do more whenever I shall believe doing more will help the cause.

A different emphasis can, however, be found elsewhere.

Whatever may be said about his attitude to slavery, in Lincoln's eyes the cause of the Union and the cause of world democracy were inseparable. The triumph of the one was the triumph of the other. The closing words of the Gettysburg oration must be repeated – 'We here highly resolve that these dead shall not have died in vain; that this nation, under God, shall have a new birth of freedom; and that government of the people, by the people, for the people, shall not perish from earth'. Here a devotion to freedom is surely attributed to both sides in the struggle; the final words are rounded off with the glorious expression of the democratic dream of history. The unity and the democracy were to go forward hand in hand.

But the arguments for unity and for democracy do not necessarily point in the same direction. The Irish leaders who won their country's independence drew no little inspiration from Lincoln, but in the summer of 1921 they indignantly repudiated Lloyd George's attempts to invoke Lincoln's shade in support of the British case against the secession of Ireland. In Lincoln's case it was three ideals which supplied him with the invincible assurance. Unity, democracy and the ultimate extinction of slavery cannot, in the last resort, be separated, as we seek to read his mind.

A fourth ideal should be placed alongside. The conviction that if the Union were to succeed, it must be a Union of mutual trust and loyalty to which military victory was nothing more than a prelude. Lincoln rose to his greatest heights in the second inaugural, delivered in March 1865, little more than a month before he died. The North were close to victory, but they had not yet won. Thoughts and emotions were conveyed which no other conqueror can have equalled: 'Both', he said, 'read the same Bible, and pray to the same God; and each invokes His aid against the other. . . . The prayers of both could not be answered; that

220

of neither has been answered fully.' Was ever such sympathy and true understanding shown towards those who were facing utter defeat by the man who, more than any other, had defeated them? 'With firmness in the right', he concluded, 'as God gives us to see the right, let us strive on to finish the work we are in. . . .' Did anyone ever combine so strong a conviction with such complete humility?

When Lincoln left Springfield for the White House in 1861, he referred, as we have seen, to the task before him being greater than that which rested upon Washington, 'Without the assistance', he went on, 'of that Divine Being who ever attended him, I cannot succeed. With that assistance I cannot fail. Trusting in Him who can go with me and remain with you and be everywhere for good, let us confidently hope that all will yet be well. . . . To His care commending you, as I hope in your prayers you will commend me, I bid you an affectionate farewell.' An honest man who used those words might or might not wish to call himself a Christian; he revealed himself at the very least as profoundly religious. Yet one cannot believe that the allegations by Herndon and others about his earlier scepticism and his addiction to Tom Paine and Voltaire were manufactured out of nothing but malice. Two men who had known him well in earlier days, one of them, John T. Stuart – his first law partner – were dragged in at one moment to confirm the irreligious estimates of Lincoln. Both indignantly repudiated the attribution of such views to themselves, but both in doing so recorded their belief that Lincoln had been 'an infidel in the earlier part of his life'. By 1846, however, it would seem that a great change had already come about and by 1860, as can be seen from the passage quoted, his spiritual development had gone much further. The years in the White House seem to have wrought a further sublimation, not only of degree but of kind.

Shortly before his death, he said to a friend: 'When I left Springfield I asked the people to pray for me. I was not a Christian. When I buried my son, the severest trial of my life in 1862, I was not a Christian. But when I went to Gettysburg and saw the graves of thousands of our soldiers, I then and there consecrated myself to Christ.'

His religion was justified by its fruits. He was always immensely accessible. His compassion seemed to expand as the sorrows of war bore down on him more heavily. Mothers made a special appeal to him, whether their sons were fallen war heroes, or under sentence of death for cowardice. He found children irresistible –

his own, the young girl who persuaded him to grow a beard and countless others. When Lieutenant-Colonel McCullough was killed in the Vicksburg campaign, Lincoln learned that one of his daughters had become inconsolable. At Christmas time, 1862, he found time amid grave anxieties to write to Fanny McCullough: 'It is with deep grief that I learn of the death of your kind and brave father; and especially that it is affecting your young heart beyond what is common in such cases. In this sad world of ours, sorrow comes to all; and to the young it comes with bitterest agony, because it takes them unawares. The older have learned to ever expect it.' He was anxious to offer some alleviation of her present distress, though perfect relief was not possible except with time. 'You cannot', he wrote, 'now realize that you will ever feel better. Is not this so? And yet it is a mistake. You are sure to be happy again. . . . The memory of your dear father, instead of an agony, will yet be a sad sweet feeling in your heart, or a purer and holier sort than you have ever known before.'

Lincoln comes before us as a four-fold prophet – the prophet of American Union, democracy, emancipation from slavery and reconciliation after strife. He was, or became, a humanitarian in the depth of his being and a Christian of no church, or every church.

OVERLEAF Newly freed slaves in Virginia, liberated by Northern troops. Lincoln once wrote about slavery: 'As I would not be a *slave*, so I would not be a *master* – This expresses my idea of democracy – whatever differs from this, to the extent of the difference, is no democracy.' (Courtesy Chicago Historical Society)

Further Reading

Agar, Herbert, *American Presidents*, 1933

Agar, Herbert, *Abraham Lincoln*, 1952

Ballard, Colin, *Military Genius of Abraham Lincoln*, 1920

Barton, William, *The Soul of Abraham Lincoln*, 1920

Catton, Bruce, *Penguin Book of the American Civil War*, 1966

Charnwood, Lord, *Abraham Lincoln*, 1917

Churchill, Winston, *History of the English Speaking Peoples*, Vol. IV,
1958

Cunliffe, Marcus, *American Presidents and the Presidency*, 1969

Herndon, William H., *Herndon's Lincoln – the True Story of a Great Life*,
1889

Johannsen, Robert W., *Stephen A. Douglas*, 1973

Maurice, Frederick, *Statesmen and Soldiers of the Civil War*, 1926

Nicolay, John G. and Hay, John, *Abraham Lincoln: A History* (10 vols.),
1890

Randall, James R., *Lincoln the President: From Springfield to Gettysburg*,
1945

Ross, Ishbel, *The President's Wife: Mary Todd Lincoln*, 1973

Sandburg, Carl, *Abraham Lincoln: The Prairie Years* (2 vols.), 1926

Sandburg, Carl, *Abraham Lincoln: The War Years* (4 vols.), 1939

Thomas, Benjamin, *Abraham Lincoln*, 1953

Turner, Justin and Linda Levitt, *Mary Todd Lincoln – Her Life and
Letters*, 1972

Williams, T. Harry, *Lincoln and His Generals*, 1952

Acknowledgments for Photographs

The author and publishers would like to thank the following for supplying photographs: the Phoebus Picture Library for the pictures on pp. 43 (*above*), 107 (*above*) and 213; the Orbis Publishing Co. for pictures on pp. 94 (*above*), 101, 109, 112, 120–1, 145, 153, 160–1, 165 (*below*), 170–1, 178–9, 192–3 and 200–1.

Picture research by Philippa Lewis

Maps designed by Design Practitioners Ltd

Index

Adams, Francis, 117
Alabama, 117–18
Albert, Prince, of England, 117, 212, 215
Armstrong, Jack, 20, 59
Armstrong, William, 59
Army, Confederate, 135–6, 148, 156–8, 162, 182, 197–8, 203; of the Potomac, 109–10, 126, 134, 152, 182; Union, 100–1, 105, 108, 110, 122, 126, 141, 144, 148–9, 157
Atlanta, 186, 189

Banks, General, 161–3
Battles: Antietam 1862, 135–7, 139, 144; Bull Run 1861, 100, 105, 109, 163, 186; Chancellorsville 1863, 152, 156; Chattanooga 1863, 168; Chickamauga 1863, 162–3; Fair Oaks 1862, 128; Fredericksburg 1862, 149; Gettysburg 1863, 105, 156–7, 162, 168; Manassas 1862, 137; Nashville 1864, 190; Seven Days 1862, 128–9, 132; Shiloh 1862; 124, 186; Vicksburg 1863, 125, 149, 158–62, 168, 223
Beauregard, General, 105
Bedell, Grace, 92
Booth, John Wilkes, 204
Bragg, General, 162
Breckinridge, John, 85
Brooks, Noah, 156, 194, 196
Brown, John, 74, 79
Burnside, General, 149, 152–3, 157

Cabinet, 88, 90, 99, 111, 117, 137, 178, 185–6, 193, 198, 203
California, 47, 64
Carpet-baggers, 211
Cartwright, Peter, 46
Cass, Lewis, 21
Chattanooga, 162–3
Chase, Salmon, 79–80, 88–9, 112, 129, 135, 159, 183, 185
Chicago, 54, 60, 65, 79, 186, 188
Cincinnati, 60–1, 89

Civil War, 21, 44, 46, 76, 110, 139, 186, 212, 218–19
Clay, Henry, 40–1, 54, 64 67, 74, 79
Confederates, 91, 105, 113–14, 116–17, 126, 132, 135, 137, 149, 156, 160, 168, 180, 182, 190–2, 203
Congress, 21, 32, 40, 45–7, 54, 66–8, 70, 100, 109–13, 175, 180, 186, 189, 191, 203, 211, 219
Conkling, James, 175

Davis, David, 56, 58
Davis, Jefferson, 91, 139, 190, 197, 211
Democrats, 22, 40–1, 52, 65, 67–8, 70–1, 79, 85, 88, 110–11, 114, 140, 148, 175, 178, 188
Douglas, Stephen, 64–5, 67–71, 79, 85, 97, 218
Douglass, Frederick, 196

Early, General, 186
East, the, 77, 125, 149, 162, 186
Emancipation, 46, 69, 136, 148
Everett, Edward, 168, 173

Ford's Theatre, 203
Fort Sumter, 91, 97, 99–100
Francis, Simeon, 29
Frémont, John, 113

Garrison, William Lloyd, 45
Georgia, 162, 190
Gettysburg Address, 59, 173–4, 194, 220, 222
Gladstone, William, 12, 24, 139
Grant, Ulysses, 110, 113, 122, 124, 133, 149, 158–63, 178, 180, 182, 185–6, 190, 194, 196–8
Great Britain, 100, 117–18, 212
Greeley, Horace, 74, 136, 220

Halleck, General, 110, 128, 133, 136, 152, 157–9, 162
Hanks, Dennis, 17, 90
Hanks, John, 18, 77, 218

Halstead, Murat, 159
Harpers Ferry, 74, 135
Henry, Anson, 29
Herndon, William, 21, 23–4, 26–8,
    36, 54–9, 61, 66–9, 74, 76, 88,
    91–2, 222
Hooker, General Joseph, 149, 152–3,
    157

Illinois, 13, 18, 22, 27, 37, 40, 45, 47,
    54, 59, 64, 67–8, 74, 77, 173
Indiana, 16–18

Jackson, Andrew, 40–1
Jackson, Stonewall, 127–8, 132,
    134–5, 153, 157
Johnston, General, 105, 127–8,
    159–60

Kansas–Nebraska Bill, 65, 67–8
Keckley, Elizabeth, 114
Kentucky, 13, 16–17, 27, 29–30, 85,
    99, 114, 189

Lee, Robert E., 101, 105, 110, 127–8,
    134–6, 148–9, 152–3, 156–8, 162,
    182, 194, 197–8, 210–11
Lexington, 27
Lincoln, Abraham, birth, 12–13;
    education, 16–17; in New Salem,
    18, 20–2; early romances, 22–4; at
    Springfield, 24–6; and his wife,
    27–30, 32, 36, 46–7, 114, 116, 190;
    and his children, 32, 46–7, 116,
    196; and slavery, 41, 45–6, 68–71,
    136–7, 141, 144; as a congressman,
    47, 52–4; withdraws from politics,
    55–61; returns, 66–8; prepares for
    Presidency, 74, 76–7, 79–80;
    becomes President, 85; and his
    Cabinet, 88–90; goes to
    Washington, 91–2, 97; and
    secession, 97–100; policy during
    Civil War, 101, 105, 108–13, 122
    124, 126–8, 132–5, 144, 149, 152,
    157–62, 180, 186; and Great
    Britain, 117; and Gettysburg
    Address, 156, 168, 173–4; attempts
    to make peace, 175, 178, 190–4,
    197–8; attitudes to, 183, 185, 208–
    12, 215; re-election, 188–90, 195–
    6; assassination, 203–4, 208;
    summing-up, 218–20, 222–3
Lincoln, Edward 'Eddie', 32, 46

Lincoln, Nancy, 12–13
Lincoln, Mary, 27–30, 32, 46–7, 64,
    88, 92, 113–14, 116, 189–90, 196,
    203, 208, 212, 215
Lincoln, Robert, 30, 32, 208
Lincoln, Sarah, 13, 17–18, 91
Lincoln, Thomas, 12–13, 17–18, 91
Lincoln, Thomas, 'Tad', 32, 114, 116,
    196, 208
Lincoln, William, 'Willie', 32, 114,
    196, 203
Logan, Stephen, 26
Lyons, Lord, 116–17

Maryland, 99, 135–6, 162, 204
McClellan, General George, 109–12,
    125, 127–9, 132, 134–6, 144,
    148–9, 152, 159, 162, 182, 186, 189
McDowell, General Irvin, 105, 108–9,
    126–7
Meade, General, 157–8, 162, 173, 196
Merrimac, 129, 132
Mexico, 46, 52, 64; War 1846–7, 47,
    54, 110, 122
Mississippi River, 37, 109, 113, 125,
    149, 162–3
Missouri, 99, 113
Missouri Compromise 1820, 44, 64,
    70
Monitor, 130

New Orleans, 18, 125, 218
New Salem, 18, 20–4, 46, 59, 88, 99
New York, 74, 77, 79, 186, 211
North, the, 44, 64, 67, 71, 74, 91,
    99–100, 105, 109, 113, 116, 122,
    125, 128, 137, 139, 149, 157, 162,
    168, 178, 195, 220

Offutt, Denton, 18, 20–1
Owens, Mary, 24, 27–8

Palmerston, Lord, 116–17, 137
Pemberton, General, 159–60
Pennsylvania, 80, 88, 136, 156–7,
    162
Peoria Address, 68–9, 71, 218
Pickett, Thomas, 74
Pope, General, 110, 134–5, 153, 157

Rathbone, Major, 203–4
Representatives, House of, 45, 64
Republicans, 67, 70–1, 79, 85, 111,
    113, 140, 175, 173, 185, 211, 219

Richmond, 105, 110, 121, 127, 129, 132, 135, 144, 157, 182, 196–7
Rosecrans, General, 162
Russell, Lord John, 116–17, 137, 139
Rutledge, Ann, 22–4

Scallywags, 211
Scott, Dred, 70, 79, 85
Scott, General, 101, 105, 108, 110
Senate, 36, 64–5, 69–70, 79, 194
Seward, William, 79–80, 88, 111, 114, 116–17, 173, 191, 197
Sheridan, General, 189
Sherman, General, 186, 189–90, 196, 203
Shields, James, 36–7
Slavery, 41, 44–6, 64, 66–71, 74, 76–7, 79–80, 91, 112, 114, 136, 178, 195, 218–20, 223
Smith, Caleb, 88
South, the, 41, 45, 64, 66, 71, 74, 76, 80, 85, 98–9, 109, 112, 114, 116, 128, 139, 149, 157, 168, 175, 178, 190, 195, 204, 211–12, 219
South Carolina, 41, 91, 218
Speed, Joshua, 18, 24–6, 29
Springfield, 18, 22, 24, 26–9, 32, 40, 47, 55, 68, 76–7, 80, 85, 88, 91, 208, 222
Stanton, Edwin, 60–1, 89–90, 128–9, 132–3, 159, 180, 194, 197
Stephens, Alexander, 191
Stuart, John, 22–5, 222

Sumner, Senator, 36
Swett, Leonard, 18

Taney, Chief Justice, 70
Taylor, General, 54
Thomas, Benjamin, 24, 26, 55, 60, 136
Trent, 117–18

Union, the, 45, 65, 67, 71, 74, 85, 91, 97–100, 105, 109–10, 113–14, 116, 135–6, 140, 149, 163, 168, 175, 178, 186, 189–90, 198, 203, 218–19, 223

Victoria, Queen of England, 117, 212, 215
Virginia, 59, 102, 105, 109, 134, 136, 182, 197, 204

War Department, 105, 158, 162–3, 203
Washington, 47, 53–5, 91–2, 105, 108–11, 114, 117, 126, 127–8, 132, 134–5, 173, 178, 185–6, 196, 198
Webster, Daniel, 41, 67, 74, 79
West, the, 44, 64, 70, 113, 125, 128, 149, 158, 160, 162
Whigs, 22, 36, 40–1, 47, 52, 54, 64, 67–8, 79, 85
White House, 108, 111, 113–14, 173, 178, 190, 196, 198, 203–4, 208, 222